D1245860

Diamonds
in the Rough

Homilies and Reflections
on the Mystery of Suffering

Sister Paula Jean Miller, FSE, Editor

En Route Books and Media, LLC
5705 Rhodes Avenue
St. Louis, MO 63109

Library of Congress Control Number: 2017963088

ISBN-10: 0-9996670-4-1
ISBN-13: 978-0-9996670-4-0

DEDICATION

To Bishop Raymond Lessard,
who in his retirement spent 20 years assisting
at St. Vincent de Paul Regional Seminary,
forming shepherds after the heart of Christ.

(December 21, 1930 – January 3, 2016)

ACKNOWLEDGMENTS

Monsignor David L. Toups, President-Rector of St. Vincent de Paul Seminary, for his personal guidance and involvement in this project, a symbol of his leadership as shepherd of the Seminary Community.

Sister Paula Jean Miller, F.S.E., Professor of Moral Theology, for encouraging us to create a class publication and editing it to final form.

Deacon Daniel Daza-Jaller, for coordinating the collection of all materials and giving the work its initial form.

Dr. Sebastian Mahfood, OP, Professor of Interdisciplinary Studies and Vice-President of External Affairs, Holy Apostles College & Seminary, and his staff for their enthusiasm and alacrity in presenting this work for the spiritual growth of the Faithful.

CONTENTS

Preface

Diamonds in the Rough is a compendium of homilies addressing the universality of human suffering in light of St. Pope John Paul II's apostolic letter *Salvifici Doloris*. The contributing seminarians express their estimations of the mysteries of suffering and of why God permits it (HASSELL, WILLIFORD, ELANGO), mirroring questions that we as Christians also ask. The missionary disciples propose insights for coping with and interpreting human suffering through the transformation of deep physical, mental and emotional pain into "a pilgrimmage to our eternal home...[to] make something good out of" it (IBEH).

Suffering is tenacious, "the result of a missing piece of what we, as humans, seek...it separates our wholeness" (SHEHAN). Yet, when we unify ourselves with other sufferers (BRITTON), each of us receives the opportunity to "share the suffering of Christ in each nook and cranny of human existence" (MILLER).

A theme of hopefulness permeates *Diamonds in the Rough* (HASSELL, TURCOTTE, AYUBI, BARROS). We sufferers pray for deliverance, for perseverance, for enlightenment in our suffering. We learn that by uniting our personal sufferings to those of Christ on the cross, our fears and anguish become "a bridge, rather than an obstacle...without meaning and purpose" (MILLER). In this manner, we are never alone (TURCOTTE, GOMEZ). Christ bestows dignity and merit on our shared suffering (BRITTON).

I join diverse readers who will mine gems of hope in the midst of suffering from *Diamonds in the Rough*. As a nurse, I find it adds another viable tool to my arsenal of empathetic caregiving for patients who suffer. As a wife, I find it has granted me retrospective reassurance about my beloved husband's grave suffering for months last year following invasive surgery. And as a patient myself many times over, I find it has helped me understand suffering as a source of hope in communion with Christ's own suffering. We need not consider suffering the end product. This book, *Diamonds in the*

Rough, encourages our acceptance of the mystery of suffering, inviting those who suffer to become participants in God's redemptive love.

Diane Haight, RN, BIS, MA

Foreword

"I had a good day."

Consider! Usually this sentence means that the speaker had a day without many annoyances or crosses.

What would you think if someone meant, instead, a day full of crosses, even tragedies, during which she or he found spiritual joy by uniting that suffering with the Cross of Jesus?

I have a friend who suffers lots of chronic physical pain, every day. When I meet her at daily Mass and I ask her how she is doing, she always smiles and says, "I am good with God."

So, how do we move from trying to avoid all pain and suffering like the plague, and if we have to endure it, responding with bitterness, to the holy response to inescapable pain characteristic of the saints?

To get a clue, keep reading *Diamonds in the*

Rough. You might not think that you could get fresh insights on this subject from one writer after another. But you would be wrong.

In my case, the author of a big book called *Avoiding Bitterness in Suffering: How our Heroes the Saints found Peace amid Sorrow*, I still found more hope from reading the little chapters in this book.

How come? I think it is because we always need more voices telling us the story of the love of Jesus for us, redeeming our sufferings.

Many of the writers in *Diamonds in the Rough* are seminarians. We know that to want to be a priest in our times of such hedonistic pleasure-seeking is in itself a choice for suffering. Some of you will resonate in a different way with the chapters by women students of theology.

To conclude this foreword, let me give you two of my best ways of teaching about suffering.

The first is from a Romanian Lutheran pastor, Richard Wurmbrand, who endured torture in a Communist prison for many years. He wrote that it all came down to whether a Christian wants to be a customer or a disciple. The customer goes to Jesus only to ask for favors. The disciple wants to be like Jesus.

The second is from experience: pain weans us from the world to long for a heaven of perfect happiness in union with God for all eternity.

Ronda Chervin, Ph.D.

Professor Emerita of Philosophy, Holy Apostles College and Seminary, author of numerous books about Catholic living, and presenter on EWTN.

Introduction

"Insofar as man becomes a sharer in Christ's
sufferings—in any part of the world and at any time
in history—to that extent *he in his own way
completes* the suffering through which Christ
accomplished the Redemption of the world."
(*Salvifici Doloris,* 24)

St. John Paul II, an evangelizer and exemplar
of the meaning and purpose of human suffering—as a participation and sharing in the redemptive mission of Jesus Christ—here lays
bare the Christian Mission of Redemptive
Suffering. John Paul II builds upon St. Paul's
insight into the mystery of the Corporate Body
of Christ—what you do to one another you do
to me—and upon the revelation of "DIVINE
LOVE *pro nobis*" (not retribution nor ven-
geance) that Paul knows animates God's re-
incorporation of humanity into Divine Relationship IN and THROUGH the Son. In com-
plement to St. Paul's theology that opens salvific glory to human participation, St. John
Paul II humbly, but definitively, specifies how

9

humanity contributes its "widow's mite" to the Trinity's salvific act: "insofar as" and "to the extent" that *each person in his or her own way completes Christ's suffering, through which Christ accomplished the Redemption of the world!* It is not enough for the God of LOVE to suffer and die *for us;* it is not enough that the Resurrected Body of Christ is constituted by the Perfect Man, Jesus Christ. By identification in his Person with each and every human being in weakness, in suffering, in all the poverties of the human condition; in his absolute identi-fication with, and in his total self-gift in love for us, Jesus Christ offers us the choice to rise above and beyond the depths into which we sink, to become "in Christ" SUFFERING LOVE *"for others,"* and in doing so to complete the Divine Circle of Salvation. Christ creates a "place" for us in his Kingdom, a unique time and space to complete Christ's suffering in a way that "has my name on it." Christ gives each of us the privilege to offer to the Father in him the "pearl of great price;" my "crown jewel": *my personal suffering* joined to his own. St. John Paul II concludes: "Yes, it seems to be part *of the very essence of Christ's redemptive suffering* that this suffering requires to be unceasingly completed." (*SD*, 24) Christ's suf-fering is completed only when united through love with the suffering of every person for whom Christ personally suffered and died.

To bring this message, invitation, and mission to every person who suffers (and who does not?) is the work of the Missionary Disciple in the New Evangelization. It is to proclaim the Gospel of Suffering—the *Good News of Suffering* to a world that has closed its ears and hardened its heart to that Word, preferring instead to remain and to die in autonomy, control, and isolation because we simply cannot believe such Good News of Unconditional Love. It is Good News that can only be brought to one person at a time by another person, who has been awakened and chosen by Christ through personal suffering. Each of us is called and chosen as a Christian to make the Suffering Christ present and available to each Beloved of God—in every part of the world and at every time in history. Together these *three persons*: 1) the one who cries out in despair and anger, "Why me? Why now? What is the meaning and purpose of this horrific experience?"; 2) the Missionary Disciple, the ambassador of Christ, who like the Good Samaritan comes to "unleash love" by simply being "with" and joining into the human question: "Why, God? What is the meaning and purpose? How can you be a

God of Love?"; and 3) the Christ: "He had no form or charm to attract us, no beauty to win our hearts; he was despised, the lowest of men, a man of sorrows, familiar with suffering, one from whom, as it were, we averted our gaze, despised, for whom we had no regard. Yet ours were the sufferings he was bearing, ours the sorrows he was carrying, while we thought of him as someone being punished and struck with affliction by God, whereas he was being wounded for our rebellions, crushed because of our guilt: the punishment reconciling us fell on him, and we have been healed by his bruises." (*Is* 53:2-5) "My God, my God, why have you abandoned me?"

To prepare this kind of Missionary Disciple of the New Evangelization is the work of human, spiritual, pastoral, and intellectual formation at St. Vincent de Paul Regional Seminary in Boynton Beach, Florida, and ultimately the work of the entire Church. To be a Missionary Disciple is to share the suffering of Christ in each nook and cranny of human existence, in order to find in each unique, personal experience of suffering the "common ground," the touchstone that reveals the meaning and purpose of human existence as a journey into becoming One Body in Christ. Ultimately, that

One Christ is a glorified existence, but always glorified in its WOUNDS, wounds that are borne in common and shared. It is into this experience of the priesthood of Jesus Christ that St. Vincent de Paul Regional Seminary strives to form men to be bridges between the inchoate suffering of humanity and the Redeemed Humanity of the Risen Christ. It is only by claiming the unique personal suffering that is involved in surrendering to the human, spiritual, pastoral, and intellectual transformation of a man into a Missionary Disciple that a priest of Jesus Christ is formed. It is only through Christ, with Christ, and in Christ that one becomes free to shape human choices that identify with and express Christ the Suffering Servant—choices that make one into a bridge, rather than an obstacle, for the one who suffers without meaning and purpose.

This book of homilies and reflections on the mystery of human suffering, in the apostolic letter of St. John Paul II, took form midway through a course in Medical Ethics for our fourth-year students. The assignment was intended as a practical exercise through which the students could "translate" St. John Paul II's theology of suffering into the life experience of parishioners as they confronted suffering and death. God, however, intended for his "little flock" a deeper, more intensely personal look at the world of medical ethics and the theology of human suffering. Within days of their theological reflections, I was plucked from their classroom for emergency surgery, followed by a month of hospitalization for infections, complications, and further surgery. As I contemplated medical ethics, suffering, and the imminent possibility of death from my hospital bed, my medical ethics class assumed responsibility for actualizing the daily modules specifying research and presentation of topics, as well as for compiling and completing their book of homilies and reflections. Our initial projections for this little book were to distinguish between pain and human suffering; between the patient's "right" to control medical treatment versus the real physical, psychological, and spiritual limits to question treatments and benefit/burden ratios; and between the "cry of Job" in every suffering human being and Christ's unfathomable invitation to become a co-redeemer of the world with him, by supplying through personal sufferings what was lacking in Christ's own sufferings. Our initial projections became a small "window" through which we were enabled to catch a glimpse of the Divine-human mystery of Suffering.

As the one "chosen" to peer through that window "up close and personal," the introduction to *human* suffering came through the excruciating *pain* that pressed me to surrender my body unequivocally to the care of an anonymous army of hospital services that probed, prodded, transported, examined, and invasively treated me; this technological anonymity and indignity was daily softened by particular doctors and nurses whose faithful care was personal and relational. The psychological fantasy that sustained me through the first week of hospitalization was that in a few days I would be back home, on my feet, going about all my responsibilities with my usual energy and dispatch. However, after an early discharge, quick relapse and expedited ER admit, my physical, emotional, mental and spiritual condition exploded my psychological myth. My body's violent resistance to the insertion of a nasal-gastric tube (required for the next several weeks to preserve my life), left me face-to-face with the question of my readiness for death and the re-examination of my understanding of life, of meaning, consecration, and mission to the Church and world. While my Religious Community and Seminary clergy supported me in my interior spiritual struggle, particularly through the Eucharist and repeated Anointing, any ambiguity in my thinking was met with firm resistance from our seminary Rector, who repeatedly asserted that "dying is not an option." This stage of spiritual struggle became my entrance point into human suffering as co-redemptive, now not as a theologian but as a limited, created person. As the subsequent weeks of hospitalization wore on me, the "horizontal" line of treatments led neither to healthy resumption of life nor to transformation through death into eternal life, but only to an endless sequence of fixings that opened to new obstacles. At that point, a third option for Church ministry suggested itself to me: not death; not life and ministry as I had known it; but a ministry of suffering for the Church like the one I was then being asked to live. Opening myself to that option was the most difficult "yes," but one that revealed human life as a fragile gift, received from the Hand of God and returned to him each day; a gift that sustains us in our daily choices to participate in Divine Love, in Joy, and yes, in Suffering.

The prayer of Mary, the *Theotokos*: "Be it done unto me according to thy Word" begins the liturgical year of the Church in Advent. The prayer of her Son, Jesus the Christ: "Abba, Father, all things are possible to you. Take this cup away from me, but not what I will but what you will" (Mk 14:36) begins Lent: Passion/ Death/and Resurrection—the New Creation of the Second Adam and the New Eve. Between these two self-offerings of the New Eve and the New Adam—these two prayers of total dispon- ability to the Will of the Father—lies the world of human choice, the mystery of human suf- fering, death, and the glorified life of the New Created Order. It is through and within the world of human choices that persons are called by God to conform their lives to Jesus Christ through the discipline of mutual, faithful relationship; to train bodies, senses, imagi- nations, thoughts, affections, wills, and spirits to *follow as disciples*. Gradual configuration to Christ causes the sentiments and attitudes of the Son of God to arise in the life of the disciple; re-creating us in the likeness of the Good Shepherd.

The key to understanding formation of future priests at St. Vincent de Paul Regional Semi- nary is the formation of men—humanly, spiri- tually, pastorally, and intellectually—as Mis- sionary Disciples of Jesus Christ who share in his Shepherd's heart. As Monsignor David Toups explains in his *Reclaiming our Priestly Character,* "The priest has been sealed and ontologically changed through ordination for a specific purpose: so that he can make Christ sacramentally present to the faithful."[1] But the Church calls a seminarian to be *both* 1) configured to Christ the Head, the Divine Bridegroom—ontologically changed through Ordination into the likeness of the Good Shepherd who lays down his life for the Church *and* 2) to become one with Christ's Bride, the Church, in and through the Eucharist they celebrate. As each member pledges "Amen" to being "concorporated" with every other member in Christ's Body, he/she also assumes the subsequent moral responsibility to live the one commandment of Christ: "Love one another as I have loved you."[2] During his time in the seminary (i.e., the "seedbed"), the "seed" of *personal identity* must undergo death in order to rise again as a *Spousal Priestly Identity*, an identity constituted by a life commitment to Inter-Personal RELATION that both capacitates the priest to be the "presence sacrament" of Jesus Christ, the Bridegroom for his Bride,

---

[1] Toups, Father David, *Reclaiming Our Priestly Character*, IPF Publications: Omaha, NE, 2008, 155.

[2] See Livio Melina, *The Epiphany of Love: Toward a Theological Understanding of Christian Action*, William B. Eerdmans Publishing Company: Grand Rapids, Michigan/Cambridge, U.K., 2010.

and enables the priest to be a con-corporated member *of the Bride,* to present her *in his priestly person* as an acceptable Eucharistic sacrifice to her Bridegroom. In a word, the Catholic Seminary is missioned to prepare priests to become *Men of Communion* with the marginalized, isolated, suffering, and abandoned, so that "consecrated through the offering of Jesus Christ once for all" they may respond to Christ: "a body you prepared for me; Behold I come to do your will!" (Hebrews 10:5-7)

Sister Paula Jean Miller, FSE
December 8, 2017

Feast of the Immaculate Conception of Mary,
Mother of God

1

Rev. Mr. Daniel Daza-Jaller

Once as kids, my brother and I were in one of our usual fights. As I closed in on him, and he ran into the bathroom and slammed the door shut! Unfortunately, my finger was in the jam of the door as it came to a close. Needless to say, the finger was not a pretty sight. After cleaning me up, my mother took me to the doctor to make sure all was ok. On the ride there, I could feel my finger burning and throbbing. After examining my finger, the doctor asked: "Is it throbbing at all?" I was convinced that if I said yes she would do something which would make it hurt more. So, I looked up at her and said: "Of course not!"

How often we do this with our own sufferings and pains! We have all experienced deep suffering and pain; much deeper than a jammed finger. These wounds cause our entire being to burn and throb, calling for attention to be healed. Out of fear of the pain of healing, or perhaps out of shame, or anger, or disbelief, we refuse to reveal our wounds to the doctor. We refuse to reveal the depths of our aches and our agony. But the Lord, He who is the divine physician, invites and begs us to bring our pains and sufferings to Him.

Jesus desires not only to heal us, but more deeply to unveil to us the cause, the reason, the purpose, and the very meaning of our suffering. (cf. *Salvifici Doloris*, 9.1) This process to which the divine physician invites us does not happen overnight; it is not an "out-patient procedure," nor does it necessarily rid us of all pain and suffering. Jesus invites us to a deeper understanding of our pain, so that we can bear it with love.

He wants to rid us of all fear and aversion to pain and suffering. He reminds us that He did this in His own earthly life as He approached Jerusalem with full consciousness of what He would have to endure there, and He is able to approach it with courage due to the fact that He saw this suffering within the context of the mission of salvation; (cf. *SD*, 16f) Jesus today offers this to us. He wants to assure us that if we face our sufferings with Him and in Him, if we approach them under the "light of salvation," (*SD*, 15.3) we will be given a share in the continuing redemptive act of His own suffering. He promises us that our own suffering, an experience of evil in the world, can introduce goodness into the world, in the same way that His suffering on the Cross brought about the ultimate good, the glory of the Resurrection, the reward of eternal life for all.

This recognition and acceptance of suffering is not easy. Just bringing it to Jesus, our divine physician, can seem extremely difficult. This is not only our experience, but the experience of the saints throughout the history of the Church, down to the first apostles. Mary, our sorrowful Mother, is here with us. She accompanies us at the foot of the Cross and helps us to embrace the suffering Christ as He embraces our own suffering. (cf. Jn. 19:25-27) May we look to Mary to help us daily, not to run or hide from our suffering and pain, but to embrace it, so that in union with that of Christ, it too may be transformed into glory for the salvation of all.

Deacon Daniel Daza-Jaller is a seminarian of the Diocese of Palm Beach in his last year of formation at St. Vincent de Paul Regional Seminary. A native Colombian, he immigrated to the US with his family when he was eight years old. After graduating high school, he spent a year abroad as an exchange student. On August 6, 2009, on the Feast of the Transfiguration of the Lord, he began his seminary formation. He graduated St. John Vianney College Seminary in May, 2013. With the grace of God, he will be ordained a priest on May 5, 2018.

2

Rev. Mr. Chris Hassel

There is no doubt that suffering exists in our lives. We deal with it throughout our lives, with the loss of loved ones, illnesses, and diseases that we experience personally or through someone else, and other hardships that present themselves in life. And these sufferings can be a mystery that we can enter into or not. If we look at the life of Mary, the mother of Jesus, we can see how she entered into the mystery by entering into the suffering of her son through her own suffering. She united her suffering with that of Jesus. As Saint Pope John Paul II said of Mary, "from the time of her secret conversation with the angel, she began to see in her mission as a mother her 'destiny' to share... in the very mission of her Son." (*Salvifici Doloris*, 25) Mary's knowledge of the suffering she would face grew from the time of Jesus' birth through the pronouncement of Simeon, that her heart would be pierced by a sword. And as Jesus began his ministry, she was ever aware of the ever increasing suffering her Son endured as he moved closer to the Cross. It was at the Cross that her suffering and understanding would come to its height. (cf. *SD*, 25)

It is through entering into the mystery of the suffering that we are experiencing that we find more can be brought to us when we unite our suffering with Christ's. Christ's suffering was as human as our suffering, for he was human in every way but sin. However, in Christ's suffering salvation was brought about for us all. His suffering was for the redemption of humanity. He came because of the great love of the Father for us; such great love it was that He sent His only begotten Son into the world to die for our salvation. We see that love Christ has for us in the Scriptures, as Christ would minister always to those suffering around him: the poor, the sick, those on the fringes of society. Christ is close to those who are suffering. And it is in our suffering, when we enter into it and unite it with Christ's suffering, that we find that great love of Christ. It is in this that we become susceptible to the power of God, the salvific power of the Cross of Christ. That is to say when we enter into our suffering and unite it with Christ, we find and receive perseverance and hope. In the mystery of suffering, we find that when our suffering is united with Christ's suffering, we have the hope that maintains us so that the suffering will not get the best of us nor deprive us of our own dignity.

This is the example that Mary has for us all. Her suffering was united with the suffering of Christ. (cf. *SD*, 25) And suffering is difficult; there is no doubt in this. It is not easy, nor was it easy for Mary to see her Son suffer. Yet her suffering did not pull her away, away from Christ; she moved into her suffering and united her suffering with Christ, where she found hope, love, and the redemption that Christ brought to the world. (cf. *SD*, 25) When we unite our suffering with Christ, we find hope, strength, and redemption; we find our own dignity and our mission to follow Christ.

Deacon Chris Hassel is a seminarian of the Diocese of Savannah, GA. Originally from Ohio, he received a Bachelor of Science (B.S.) in Computer Science from Bowling Green State University, in Bowling Green, OH, in 2002 and a Master of Arts in Philosophical Studies from Mount St. Mary's University, Emmitsburg, MD, in 2013. He also spent time in the United States Air Force as a Communications Officer. Presently in his final year of Theology at St. Vincent de Paul Regional Seminary, in Boynton Beach, Deacon Chris will be ordained to the priesthood upon his graduation in June, 2018.

3

Rev. Mr. Lou Turcotte

Reflection based on the readings for Thursday of the Twenty-ninth Week in Ordinary Time (*Romans* 6:19-23; *Psalm* 1:1-6; *Luke* 12:49-53)

The word "Gospel" means "good news," but today that doesn't really feel like it's the case. Jesus speaks of the division caused by His arrival on earth, a division that can even tear apart families. Maybe some of you have already experienced something like that in your lives. Often, because of our faith, because of our relationship with Christ, we can feel a distance creep in between old friends, co-workers, and even certain members of our family. Sometimes it goes beyond a feeling; sometimes the division is real, and we are cut off from those we love because they do not wish to follow Christ alongside us. This division is painful; it is a unique kind of suffering.

Suffering can take many different forms, but it is something that we all experience. In the mid-80's, Pope John Paul II wrote to the Church about this very truth, and in it, he referred to the Bible as "a great book about suffering," listing the many painful experiences described in Scripture; suffering to which many of us can relate: sickness, the death of a loved one, persecution, mockery, loneliness, abandonment, remorse, injustice, and, yes, the conflict, infidelity, and division encountered with those closest to us. The heroes of Scripture, like us today, discover first-hand how difficult life can be in a fallen world.

But it is this difficult life, this fallen world, in which God has become man. When Jesus entered into this world, He entered into every part of it and took on our suffering and pain in a real and intimate way. He too experienced the pain of persecution, the ache of abandonment, the sting of death. But He didn't just accept it; the Gospel today tells us He longed for it. He longed for the baptism of His suffering and death because He knew that the same suffering and death would bring about resurrection and redemption, for all of us. And this, my friends, is the "good news" of today's Gospel. Not only can we be consoled in knowing that we are never alone in our sufferings, that Christ knows our pain and helps us to carry it, but we also discover something new: hope.

Because of Christ's suffering, we have hope that our suffering is also redemptive; it is the very road that will lead us to salvation, lead us to everlasting life. We have hope that when it seems like nothing is going our way, maybe we are closer to our goal than ever before. We can have hope that the same faith that can cause division here on earth can also heal all wounds and lead us to profound love in the next. So today, as we come up to receive our Lord in the Eucharist, I invite us to bring with us our broken relationships, our disappointments, our weaknesses, our suffering—and allow Jesus to enter in, to transform and redeem that suffering. And then, we can echo the words we prayed in the psalm today: "Blessed are we who hope in the Lord." And that, my friends, is good news.

Deacon Lou Turcotte is a seminarian studying for the diocese of St. Petersburg, FL. Born and raised in Clearwater, FL, Deacon Lou attended the University of Florida and graduated in 2011 with a B.S. in Marketing. Upon graduation he entered priestly discernment at St. John Vianney College Seminary in Miami, FL. He graduated in 2013 with a Bachelor of Arts in Philosophy, and is now attending St. Vincent de Paul Regional Seminary in Boynton Beach, FL. Currently in his final year of studies for the Master of Divinity, he will be ordained to the priesthood in May, 2018.

4

Rev. Mr. Martin Ibeh

In the world you will have trouble, but take
courage, I have conquered the world.
(*John* 16:33b)

We live in a world beset with suffering; it's a
part of our journey of life.

In the Gospel of John, Christ warns us to
expect suffering in this life, but he urges us to
"take courage, I have conquered the world."
(*John* 16:33b)

How reassuring and comforting it is to hear
these words from the Lord who loves us so
much that he himself suffered for us! How
consoling it is to hear the faithful promise of
our loving Savior who from eternity has been
working for the good of those who love him!

Suffering was never part of God's plan for us. It
came to us through our first parents, Adam and
Eve, who disobeyed God in the garden. (cf.
Rom 5: 12-14, 19) Yet, the Lord of Love did not
stop loving; the merciful Creator didn't stop re-

creating; the Lord of Life didn't stop giving life. Out of his boundless love and mercy, Christ came into the world to save us from the sting of suffering and death; he laid down his life on the cross to heal our brokenness and reclaim us.

Keep in mind that Christ didn't promise that our lives on earth would be free from suffering, but he promised his abiding, healing presence; he promised that those who put their trust in him and endure to the end will live with him in the eternal kingdom where there will be no more suffering, no more death, no more evil. In Christ, our suffering is not in vain. The Lord uses whatever adversity we may undergo to refine and strengthen us to be more like him who gave his life out of love for our salvation. He also allows suffering to remind us that we are not yet home, but on a pilgrimage, journeying towards our eternal home where we'll see God face-to-face. In Christ, life does not end here; death serves only as a gateway to endless life. We may not avoid the distress of this world, but we can avoid the despair that comes with it. We may not cure the grief that is part of this life, but we can choose to live in peace of mind and joy of heart if we fix our gaze on the cross, if we put our confidence in the Lord.

Whatever you may be passing through at this moment (sickness, abuse, rejection, persecution, poverty, loss), know that Christ is with you; he says to you personally, "Take courage!" We can learn from a little boy who placed his hand on his grieving mom and said, "Mom, trust God, for He will make something good out of it." The Lord will surely make something good out of our suffering. I may not understand fully why God allows us to experience sorrow, but I know that God's name is Love; I know that love is stronger than hurt. In his time, our merciful and compassionate Lord will turn things around for our good.

Christ has come to heal us! Today, ask him to plunge you into His river of peaceful life and give you strength to stand firm in the faith, no matter what may come your way. You can hear Him urging us to be of courage, for he has truly conquered our world of suffering and death!

 **Deacon Martin L. C. Ibeh** is a seminarian of the diocese of St. Augustine, Florida. Originally from Southeastern Nigeria, Dcn. Ibeh received the Certificate in Education (NCE) from OSISATECH College of Education, Enugu, Nigeria in 2001,

a Bachelor of Science degree (B.Sc.) from Madonna University, Okija, Nigeria, a Bachelor of Arts in Philosophy (B.A), from Kenrick-Glennon Seminary, St. Louis, MO. Presently in his final year of Theology at St. Vincent de Paul Regional Seminary, Boynton Beach, Deacon Martin will be ordained to the priesthood upon his graduation in May, 2018.

5

Rev. Mr. Misabet Garcia

In suffering, there is concealed a particular power, a special grace, that draws a person interiorly close to Christ. Certainly, with this phrase, we can understand that suffering is a reality that we as human beings cannot avoid from the time of our birth. In fact, it is significant that the first thing we do upon being born is to cry in pain, something we do not express with words. In each stage of our life, we see this reality of suffering. But, as we grow older, we come to feel it more. An example is the suffering we feel for the loss of a loved one or a terminal illness that we contract. And it is because of events like these that some of us rebel against God and blame him for all of our misfortunes, saying: "Why have you done this to us?" We would rather die than live. Our anger is so great because of the suffering we are experiencing that we do not realize that our suffering is showing us that "there is concealed a particular power that draws us interiorly closer to Christ. This is a special grace." (*Salvifici Doloris*, 26.2)

And, in effect, this special grace is a profound conversion toward God. For example, "many saints, such as Saint Francis of Assisi, Saint Ignatius of Loyola, and others, owe their profound conversion" (*SD*, 26.2) to the suffering they experienced in their lives. I know that we are not going to be saints in the same way as they were, but thanks to suffering, we are going to "discover a particular confirmation of the spiritual greatness" (*SD*, 26.2) of coming closer to God. This "spiritual greatness in suffering is certainly the result of a particular conversion and cooperation with the grace of the Crucified Redeemer" (*SD*, 26.3) who is the consoling Spirit in our lives.

Finally, we need to understand that "suffering is, in itself, an experience of evil. But Christ has made suffering the firmest basis of the definitive good, namely the good of our eternal salvation." (*SD*, 26.3) Through our suffering, Christ leads us into the Kingdom of his Heavenly Father. Today, if any of us is suffering, remember that: "Jesus Christ through his own salvific suffering on the cross is very much present in all of us."

Rev. Mr. Misabet Garcia was born and raised in Cuernavaca Morelos, Mexico. After studying engineering, he worked at IEM industries as a quality engineer at Bridgestone Firestone Industries of Mexico as supervisor of product quality, and at the University of Morelos in Cuernavaca as a teacher of mathematics, physics, and chemistry. In Mexico, he earned two Masters degrees: one in industrial engineering and the second in chemical technology. In August, 2010, Misabet studied English at UIC for one year in preparation for priestly formation, and in 2011 he began Philosophy at Mundelein Seminary. Misabet began theological studies in 2013 at St. Vincent de Paul Regional Seminary in Florida. Deacon Misabet Garcia was ordained to the diaconate for the Archdiocese of Chicago in January, 2018. He hopes to be ordained as a priest in May, 2018.

6

Rev. Mr. Maria Lucas Gunalan Joseph Elango

Suffering in itself has no ephemeral value; but when man unites his sufferings with that of Christ on the cross, he finds meaning, because through His suffering and death on the cross Christ gave life to all mankind. Through partaking in the very suffering of Christ, every man then makes his own suffering redemptive as he partakes in Christ's act of redemption.

One attitude that the Holy Father invites us to cultivate is the virtue of faith. Through deepening one's faith, a Christian discovers and gives meaning to everything that happens to him. Faith helps him to mature spiritually and to carry all his sufferings with patience and love. It gives him the assurance that God is with him, and it gives him the strength to be able to cope with the pain of suffering. Because the Christian suffers, by belonging to the Church of Christ, his sufferings are also open to redemption in Christ. In this context, the Holy Father speaks of the Gospel of Suffering; he speaks of the salvific meaning of suffering in the mission of Christ, and consequently of His Church. All of this opens us to the understanding that in the Church we discover Jesus' divine-human nature.

The apostolic letter *Salvifici Doloris* speaks of an important element within human suffering: the presence of the Ever-Virgin Mary, who was present throughout the suffering of her Son. United with the suffering of her Son, her own suffering found its meaning and purpose as well. Similarly, our suffering must be united to the suffering of Christ in the hope of the resurrection. This hope gives us courage to face various difficult situations in our lives. Our suffering can only transcend human anguish through the inner strength which Christ gives us. Rooted in Christ, we can answer any questions that may come; they can only be answered through the cross of Christ. We can firmly know and understand that Christ invites us to unite with Him through our personal crosses.

When a man, enlightened by grace, is able to penetrate into the mystery of pain, he discovers "the salvific sense of his suffering in union with Christ. This transforms the depressing feelings of anguish and fear into joy and peace. Faith in participating in the sufferings of Christ carries with it the inner certainty that the man who suffers 'completes what is lacking in the sufferings of Christ'; which, in turn, serves in the spiritual the work of redemption of Christ for the salvation of his brothers and sisters." (*SD*, 27)

It is only from a Christian perspective that it is possible to live the mystery of suffering with peace. It teaches that this suffering is not sterility but a source of redemption and trans-formation, not only of the one who suffers but the suffering of the whole world. "Suffering, more than anything else, is the one that opens the way to the grace that transforms souls. Suffering, more than anything else, makes the force of Redemption present in the history of mankind." (*SD*, 26)

We should not try to avoid pain or suffering, for it is an irreplaceable way of grace for the transformation and conversion of souls. There-fore, the suffering carried with faith, love, and patience is never in vain, but serves for the good of the Church which is in need of constant purification. It seems to me very opportune that before the conclusion, the Pope compares this theme with the passage of the Good Samaritan. The Good Samaritan not only feels compassionate towards the suffering victim, but in offering to help the suffering man, offers his help with love. Therefore, the Pope is inviting us to leave our egoism and help others to heal their pain, through an exercise of charity. Suffering should move us to be compassionate and to an experience of love in order to transform the world into a civilization of love.

Deacon Maria Lucas Gunalan is a seminarian of the Archdiocese of Kington, Jamaica, West Indies. Originally from Tamil Nadu, South India, he has his diploma in Computer Applications. He finished his canonical requirements of philosophical studies at the Pontifical Seminary of St. Thomas Aquinas, Santo Domingo, Dominican Republic. Presently in his final year of Theology at St. Vincent de Paul Regional Seminary, Boynton Beach, Deacon Lucas will be ordained to the priesthood upon his graduation in May, 2018. His Motto in Life: "In All Things Give Glory to God." "We are wounded but graced."

7

Rev. Mr. John Sollee

When it comes to suffering and evil, there is good news and there is bad news. The bad news first. Evil and suffering create a problem that is irresolvable, insurmountable. I know you want to hear good news, but we need to hear this and let it sink in. No amount of human muscle, no amount of human intellectual sophistication, no amount of personal wealth, no amount of creative ingenuity, no amount of technological advancement, no amount of political power, no amount of personal sympathy can defeat evil and end suffering. Let that sink in. We cannot save ourselves. We need a savior. If we could clear up the problem of evil and suffering ourselves to our complete satisfaction, then there would be no need for salvation.

Ok, and now for the good news!

Praised be Jesus Christ! Our Savior conquered evil and redeemed suffering. Evil is not king of the hill. Death is not the end. Suffering is not a call to hopeless isolation. Rather Divine Love emptied evil of its power and now sits atop the proverbial hill. Death is now the beginning, the doorway to eternal life. Suffering is now a call to compassionate friendship. (cf. *Salvifici Doloris,* 8)

Jesus Christ reveals a love so real, so tender, so strong that it is capable of embracing death to bring us salvation. His love is so powerful that the powers of darkness—evil, sin, and death— completely wear themselves out trying to snuff out and extinguish his love. His suffering and death gives way to resurrection. Never again are we hopelessly alone in our suffering. Jesus Christ, the Man of Sorrows, is always with us. He has given us a new capacity, a divine capacity through our baptism, to redeem suffering, to approach death with the certain hope of resurrection, and to compassionately suffer with those who suffer.

Praised be Jesus Christ! Gone are the days of the irresolvable, insurmountable problems of evil and suffering. Now grown men, like Ignatius of Antioch, yearn for death as the way to eternal life and approach it with joy. Now teenagers who, for instance, suffer painful bone cancer, like Chiara Badano, joyfully praise Jesus when their beloved hair falls out and they utter last words before death like, "Goodbye,

Mom, be happy, because I am." Now wealthy, sophisticated women, like Louise de Marillac, abandon their leisure in search of the suffering poor so that they may comfort and befriend them. Brothers and sisters, "only in the mystery of the Incarnate Word does the mystery of man take on light." (*Gaudium et Spes*, 22; cf. *SD*, 31) Only in Jesus Christ does the problem of evil and suffering become surmountable, does it become resolvable. Praised be Jesus Christ!

Deacon John Sollee is a seminarian of the Diocese of St. Augustine. Born and raised in Jacksonville, FL, he graduated from the University of Florida. After serving as a campus missionary with the Fellowship of Catholic University Students (FOCUS) at George Washington University, he entered seminary and received his Master of Arts in Philosophical Studies from Mount St. Mary's Seminary. Presently in his final year of Theology at St. Vincent de Paul Regional Seminary, John will be ordained to the priesthood upon his graduation in May, 2018.

8

Ms. Thérèse M Shehan

Have you ever had a paper cut? Ouch! Pick up a magazine or a stack of paper from the printer and one of those sheets just jumps out and bites!

Or have you ever had a toothache? That is much more intense than a paper cut. It throbs, it aches, it vibrates through our head. And it makes life unpleasant until we can get to a dentist.

Those are pains, very real, very annoying, very intense when they happen. Pain is like that. Usually, it strikes us suddenly and our first reaction is to flinch or scream out. Pain is personal. We each feel the pain of a paper cut, a toothache, an over-stretched muscle different-ly. The doctor will ask, "What does it feel like?" because he cannot feel our pain. No one can. It is ours. It is part of having a physical body with the effects of age, use, and neglect. Much pain is temporary. Modern medicine has done much to make that possible. We pop a pill, pour on some antiseptic, use an ice pack. Eventually, the pain will abate. Our body recuperates or adapts, and we go on. Or we "power through" and wait to feel better.

But pain is not suffering. Pain and suffering are two very different things. While pain affects our body, suffering is bone deep. It casts a shadow through our life that is unshakable. Suffering is the wound we carry that cannot be healed by anything earth-bound. It is at our core. Suffering is tenacious. It takes hold of us and cannot be shaken free. Saint John Paul II, in his apostolic letter *Salvifici Doloris*, says "Suffering is something still wider than sickness, more complex and at the same time still more deeply rooted in humanity itself." While pain is our own, suffering is a common, very human experience.

We each feel pain differently and through specific experiences. However, suffering is the result of a missing piece of what we, as humans, seek. Our suffering may be a broken heart that cannot mend, or a sense of inadequacy or inability to be the person we would like to be, or fear of failure, or unfulfilled dreams, or lack of acceptance and inclusion. We want something we do not or cannot have, and it wears on us. Ultimately, it is separation from wholeness and the absolute good, which is God Himself.

Suffering is universal. Every human suffers from some sorrow. What that means is we can understand others' suffering because we suffer ourselves. And because we all suffer, we can each alleviate the suffering of others.

How? By reaching out with compassion, empathy, a helping hand, a random act of kindness to every person with whom we have contact every day. Throughout the Gospels, Jesus heals the physical pain of people He meets. But He also touches them at a much deeper level. He lifts the burden of their suffering, easing the broken heart when He returns Lazarus from the dead, understanding their need for acceptance by cleansing the leper, erasing their concerns about evil by healing the demoniac.

The best example for us to follow is the story of the Good Samaritan that Jesus teaches in the Gospel of Luke. A man is traveling the road and is attacked by bandits. A priest and a Levite walk by and do nothing to help. A Samaritan comes along. Samaritans were hated and were the "other" in society of the time. They were avoided and ignored, outcasts of society. But it is a Samaritan who stops and helps this poor man. He felt sympathy for the man's wounds; but he also felt compassion for another human being who was ignored, even shunned, by others. The Samaritan didn't "feel the man's pain." He shared in his suffering because they were both outcasts and abandoned by society. The Samaritan gave a bit of himself to make that suffering less.

As Christians, we are called to bring Christ into the world and reduce the suffering of every other human being. We cannot eliminate suffering, but we can lighten another's load because we know our own suffering. Through mercy, kindness, and compassion toward every person, we can bring the experience of Christ into every life we meet.

 **Thérèse M. Shehan** has a BA in English from Caldwell College (now Caldwell University) in New Jersey and an MA in English from Seton Hall University in New Jersey. Ms. Shehan has been an educator, senior executive of Human Resources, Executive Director of a visual arts school, executive coach, consultant, and writer. She has served on numerous non-profit social service and association Boards of Directors in South Florida. Ms. Shehan is

currently a candidate for a Master of Arts in Theological Studies degree at St. Vincent de Paul Regional Seminary in Boynton Beach, Florida.

9

Rev. Mr. Matthew Gomez

Reflection on *Salvifici Doloris*, 25-27.

One of the greatest temptations we can face when we are in the face of suffering or death is thinking that we are alone. It is one of the greatest misconceptions that we can have when we think of suffering: being lonely, having the thought that we have to suffer on our own. The good news is that we do not suffer alone. God, in His infinite love, teaches us that we do not have to undergo suffering on our own.

First and foremost, God became man. He took on sinful human nature and dwelt among us. (*Phil.* 2:7) He did this for you and for me. He became man so that He can suffer and die to redeem us from our sins, to give us eternal life. Immediately, we have this connection with God because He knows suffering, He knows what it is to endure trials and tribulations; he knows what it is like to be in pain; he knows what it means to suffer. (*Mt.* 4:2, *Jn.* 11:35, *Lk.* 22:61, and many more) He knows what it feels like to stare death in the face and die. (*Lk.* 22:42) At a fundamental level, God's dwelling among us grants us peace of mind, knowing that our Creator has already undergone what awaits us.

The other way that God teaches us that we will not suffer alone is through his Son's greatest Apostle, the Blessed Virgin Mary, his mother. At the moment of Jesus' darkest hour of suffering, when all hope was lost, when he cried to his Father "Why have you abandoned me?" (*Mt.* 27:46) his Blessed Mother stands at the foot of the cross. (*Jn.* 19:25) She stood by watching her Son's execution. I can almost imagine Jesus' pain being relieved just a little bit at the heartbroken but loving gaze of his mother.

In both examples, there is this reality of self-sacrificial love. God loves humanity to such a great degree that he offered his only begotten Son to know our suffering and to die. On the other hand, Mary loved her Son so much that she did not leave his side, even in the darkest moments of his life.

This reminds me of a pastoral experience I had about two years ago. Sandra was excited to rest during the upcoming holiday weekend. During that weekend of rest she had to take her son,

Dominic, who was three at the time to the hospital because he was in a lot of pain. The initial tests came back inconclusive and he continued to be in pain. Sandra was getting frustrated. I had been told that they were in the hospital, and I visited them with my pastor. During my visit, Dominic was visibly uncomfortable and began to cry. Sandra sat on the bed; Dominic grasped his mom's finger and he fell asleep. Dominic was in pain; Sandra was suffering but in the midst of the pain and suffering Sandra offered her love for her son, and Dominic trusted his mom. They both dealt with their respective pain and suffering together.

Suffering and pain will come, but we do not need to suffer alone. If we invite Christ and his mother into our lives, into our pain, into our suffering we will be able to endure whatever trials may come.

Deacon Matthew Gomez is in his fourth year of theology at St. Vincent de Paul Regional Seminary in sunny Boynton Beach, FL. Deacon Matthew has grown to appreciate hospital ministry in his CPE (clinical pastoral education) experience and through the support of his spiritual director and formation advisor. He is a product of Catholic education, having been to Immaculate Conception (2005), Monsignor Edward Pace High School (2009), St. Thomas University (2010), and awarded a B.A. in philosophy from St. John Vianney College Seminary (2013). He is currently finishing his M.Div. He will be ordained a priest for the Archdiocese of Miami in May of 2018.

10

Rev. Mr. Omar Ayubi

I have a simple question for you; you do not need to answer it. Just think about it. Who among us gathered here today does not have a clue of what suffering and pain is? I bet we all have gone through moments in life where suffering and pain were the theme of the day, or perhaps the theme of the week or of the month. Suffering is a constant theme throughout human existence. Human beings suffer in many different ways and to different degrees, including physically, mentally, emotionally, and morally. While medicine can seek to ease physical, mental, and emotional suffering, it cannot approach moral suffering.

The Bible is largely a collection of books about suffering. The Jewish people suffer despite their election by God, and people suffer when they stray from God's election of them. Suffering is a widespread phenomenon; we all suffer, throughout the world and throughout time. Every personal instance of suffering is a small part of that greater world of suffering. So, why do we suffer? Why is there this evil? Man and/or woman suffer and wonder why, and often suffer more deeply when he or she cannot find a satisfactory answer. Pope St. John Paul II said in his apostolic letter *Salvifici Doloris* that evil obscures our vision of God, sometimes to the point of atheism, as if to say, "an almighty and benevolent God wouldn't allow this to happen, thus, God is either not almighty or not good, which means he's not God." This confusion is often a reaction to so much undeserved suffering and unpunished evil.

Ironically, the why of suffering is answered truly in Divine Love. Yes! It is a matter of love. God gives the definite answer and solution to the problem of suffering through the cross of his Son Jesus Christ. God gave his Son so that humankind might have eternal life. This giving implies suffering: God did not just send his Son; he gave his Son. Those of you who have children, try giving up a son or daughter and tell me if there is no suffering in that action; just the thought of it is painful. But Jesus came to give us eternal life, to prevent us from dying forever. In other words, Jesus saved us from the eternal and definitive suffering of being separated from God for eternity. I cannot imagine being separated from God for eternity; it is a scary thought.

Jesus not only saved us from eternal damnation, but also from our temporal suffering. He was around the sick and the suffering; He cured the leper, the blind, the lame and the deaf. He also made our individual suffering a communal suffering for his kingdom, which means suffering for others too. This participation in suffering makes us worthy of the kingdom. Because Christ identified his glory with his crucifixion, human suffering has a hidden glory in it. It is a call for moral greatness that builds spiritual character, leads to endurance and hope; thus, suffering is a call for virtue. Ultimately, personal suffering as well as the suffering of others is an invitation to love. Suffering creates an opportunity to show love, to be that "Good Samaritan." This act of love is a vocation and an apostolate when it is done genuinely from the heart.

Dear brothers and sisters, next time suffering knocks at your door, do not let fear take over; on the other hand, embrace it as Christ embraced his own suffering for love of us. I guarantee you, it will not be done in vain. The reward of embracing suffering will not only be your growth in virtue but also a sharing in the cross of Christ, our ticket to eternal life with the Father, the Son, and the Holy Spirit in the heavenly kingdom.

Dcn. Omar E. Ayubi is a seminarian of the Archdiocese of Miami, FL. Originally from Medellín-Colombia, he received a Bachelor in Computer Science from Universidad del Norte, Barranquilla, Colombia, and a Bachelor of Arts in Philosophy (B.A.) from St. John Vianney College Seminary, Miami, FL. Presently in his final year of Theology at St. Vincent de Paul Regional Seminary, Boynton Beach, FL. Deacon Omar will be ordained to the priesthood upon his graduation on May 12, 2018.

11

Rev. Mr. Gustavo Barros

All human beings, at some point in life, confront painful moments like suffering, death, sickness, and failure. Only hope in God can transform suffering into a salvific reality. As St. Paul states in his Letter to the Romans 8:18, "I consider that the suffering of this present time will not compare with the future glory that will be revealed in us."

In his apostolic letter *Salvifici Doloris,* Pope John Paul II explains that suffering seems to be, and is, almost *inseparable from man's earthly existence.* Therefore, the Church has *to try to meet man* in a special way on the path of his suffering. Suffering is something which is *still wider* than sickness, more complex, and at the same time more deeply rooted in humanity itself. A certain idea of this problem comes to us from the distinction between physical suffering and moral suffering. This distinction is based upon the double dimension of the human being and indicates that both our bodily and spiritual elements are the immediate or direct subject of suffering. Insofar as the words "suffering" and "pain" can be used, up to a certain point, interchangeably, *physical suffering* is present when "the body is hurting" in some way, whereas *moral suffering is* "pain of the soul." (*SD,* 5) People speak of their pain and suffering (sickness) as a personal story which is unexpected in their daily lives.

I remember the voice of an elderly woman who cried: "this pain is suffering." While I understood pain as in the body and suffering as spiritual, the patient—faced with her experience of suffering, pain, and frustration—an experience similar to death to itself, could find no response to the "Why has this happened to me?" question. In order to understand *the salvific meaning of suffering,* the Pope said that only by "walking in another's shoes many times" can we possibly come to understand personal suffering. Only as that person's suffering "unleashes love" and thus creates compassion in me (the ability to suffer the passion of Christ in and with the one who suffers) can I enter into the Mystery of Suffering as Co-Redemptive: "filling up what is lacking in Christ's suffering" as he allows me to participate with him in the redemption of the world.

St. John Paul II in his apostolic letter (*SD*, 9) states that the suffering endured by man, and, in fact, the whole world of suffering, inevitably raises *the question: 'Why?'* This is a question about the cause, the reason, the purpose of suffering, and, in brief, a question about its meaning. Not only does it accompany human suffering, but it seems even to determine its *human* content: what makes suffering precisely human suffering?

Personally, I had to confront this question in my own life when my uncle, who was a doctor, was assassinated in his clinic, seemingly for no reason. My world was fading away; sadness and pain immediately surged. I could not understand why they had killed my uncle of whom I was very proud. As a child, I dreamt of being a great doctor like him. There were inexplicable periods, days of uncertainty and tears because of what my family had to suffer. I came to realize in the corporate meaning of suffering and suffering "in Christ," that "if I do not suffer, I cannot help." Such is the co-redemptive meaning of human suffering.

Gustavo Barros is a Deacon for the Archdiocese of Miami. He was born in Santa Marta, Colombia, and worked in journalism for 16 years, traveling between Colombia, Miami, and Seattle. He attended the University of Miami from 2006-2008, graduating with a Master of Arts degree in journalism before attending St. John Vianney College Seminary from 2010-2013 and graduating with a Bachelor of Arts in Philosophy. Presently in his final year of theology at St. Vincent de Paul Regional Seminary, Deacon Gustavo will be ordained to the priesthood upon his graduation on May 12, 2018.

12

Rev. Mr. Tim Williford

Not too long ago, I rode in a police car with a sheriff deputy for a few hours during his shift. I work as one of their chaplains and so "ride-alongs" are how we best engage in one-on-one ministry with them. I enjoy this work so much! I tend to have some very interesting conversations with the sheriff deputies every time I go out with them. During this particular ride-along, the deputy I was with opened up to me about her Catholic upbringing as a child, but she shared with me that she wasn't currently attending Mass on Sundays. This deputy confessed her belief in God and that she even says an honest prayer before going to work each day, but it was revealed in our conversation that there was a lot about Christianity she didn't understand. For example, she thought that life was over when our mortal bodies finally give up. I was internally shocked that she didn't know of heaven or the Resurrection. She also explained to me that her husband and many of her friends aren't religious because they see so much suffering in the world and they wonder how it is possible that there can be a God when all this evil and suffering exists. In her job as a sheriff deputy, she sees evil every day.

Pope Saint John Paul II deals with this very topic in one of his apostolic letters, *Salvifici Doloris*. It's all about the meaning of human suffering. The questions raised by the friends and family of this deputy regarding why it is that suffering is present in the world and what is it that God does with suffering—is as John Paul II puts it "the question that arises from all of humanity." Isn't that so true? When unexplainable things happen to people—especially good people—we always want to know why. The answer to the question is mysterious. On one hand, we know the simple truth that sin, disordered behavior, darkness entered the world through our actions as human beings because we have the freedom to make choices against God. And those who live in the darkness seem to bring punishment on themselves—at least that's our interpretation and explanation: it goes back to the way the ancient Jewish people thought. But what about people that are good, that are innocent? When bad things happen to good people—those are the moments we find ourselves truly stumped.

These answers are only found in the mystery of God's love for us, as expressed in Jesus' willing to go the distance unto death for each and all of us; to show in his great act of love that each of us is worth it! Jesus, who is God, suffered! Jesus wept with those who suffered. When we suffer now, Jesus comes to our side to console us and to remind us of what kind of glory awaits us when we are finally able to be welcomed into the halls of heaven, where there will be no more suffering or sadness.

So why do we suffer? Why do we have to endure evil? It's because while all of creation participates to some degree in the suffering of Christ himself, *faithful* suffering with Christ will eventually end with eternal glory, just as Christ defeated death through his Resurrection. Suffering never has the last word or the final act. Only Christ is the Alpha and the Omega; the Way, the Truth, and the Life.

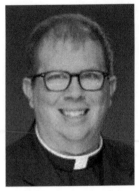

Deacon Tim Williford is a seminarian of the Diocese of St. Petersburg, Florida. Deacon Tim is a musician and worked as a church organist and choir director for eight years before entering the seminary in 2011. He earned a Bachelor of Science degree in management from the University of South Florida in Tampa, FL, in 2010. He also earned a Bachelor of Philosophy from St. John Vianney College Semi-nary in Miami. Deacon Tim is presently in his final year of Theology at St. Vincent de Paul Regional Seminary, Boynton Beach, and will be ordained to the priesthood upon his graduation in May, 2018.

13

Ms. Simi Sahu

As a fourteen-year-old who had moved less than a year prior from India to the United States, I felt cut off from all that was familiar to me and at the same time alienated from those around me. Added to the teenage angst and the usual struggles of any immigrant were the nihilistic ideas of Albert Camus and others. What began as simply adjustment troubles, spiraled downwards to an experience of deep darkness. I was also closed to hearing from my family because I was convinced that they did not understand my pain, my loss, and my sense of despair. It wasn't until one evening when my mother sat with me and wept that I realized that she did understand suffering, and my heart opened to hear her words. She related the experience of a deep loss in her life and shared what it was like to go through that suffering for years. Even so, she added that within that darkness, she had found a consoling, abiding presence and consolation that enabled her to continue to find beauty and joy in life. I could not imagine how a person who had suffered so much could give years and years of heartfelt affection to her family and genuinely give herself to her patients as a nurse at work. I went from being an angry teen who felt the world just didn't understand, to a deep realization that it was I who did not understand. I simply could not understand her ability to experience joy and love affectionately: this was alchemy, something from nothing (or whatever is worse than nothing); well beyond my understanding.

This experience led me to say my first genuine prayer. Once my mom walked away, I knelt on the floor, closed my eyes and said, "Wherever you are, whoever you are...please give me a name and a face, so that I can worship you and thank you." I had never experienced something so deep within, an aching to worship God. Two months later on my first retreat, similar to my mother's weeping eyes, I beheld the tear-filled eyes of Jesus, His face covered in tears and blood, moments before his death on a Cross. He, much more than my mother, understood suffering and offered a deep love. I had never beheld a man so beautiful, so noble, so entirely desirable as Jesus. It was like finding a prince in the gutters next to a brothel. I asked, "Lord, what are you doing here? Why would you want to come into this mess?" He answered, "I came here to be with you, because I love you."

I marveled that God loves us so much that He would find a way to suffer, just so he could be with us. Pain and suffering lead us to an isolated, dark room of loneliness and hopelessness. But Christ through His incarnation, passion, and death came to be with us, and to share with us his resurrection. I now understood why the Psalmist said, "You have turned my mourning into dancing." It is no wonder that Pope John Paul II, a man himself so acquainted with sorrow wrote in his apostolic letter, *Salvifici Doloris*:

> "In suffering there is concealed a particular power that draws a person interiorly close to Christ... A result of such a conversion is not only that the individual discovers the salvific meaning of suffering but above all that he becomes a completely new person. He discovers a new dimension, as it were, of his entire life and vocation.
>
> To the suffering brother or sister Christ discloses and gradually reveals the horizons of the Kingdom of God: the horizons of a world converted to the Creator, of a world free from sin, a world being built on the

saving power of love. And slowly but effect-tively, Christ leads into this world, into this Kingdom of the Father, suffering man, in a certain sense through the very heart of his suffering. For suffering cannot be trans-formed and changed by a grace from out-side, but from within. And Christ through his own salvific suffering is very much present in every human suffering, and can act from within that suffering by the powers of his Spirit of truth, his consoling Spirit."

As Catholics, we rejoice in our suffering, because we have found within it the presence of our tender Lord and Savior. Is it any wonder then that celibate men teach of the most passionate love the world has ever known or that the martyrs cloaked in red tell us of life eternal? No, not at all.

This is why the Psalmist, anticipating Jesus, could say:

"Whither shall I go from thy Spirit?
  Or whither shall I flee from thy presence?
If I ascend to heaven, thou art there!
  If I make my bed in Sheol, thou art there!
If I take the wings of the morning
  and dwell in the uttermost parts of the sea,

even there thy hand shall lead me,
    and thy right hand shall hold me.
If I say, "Let only darkness cover me,
    and the light about me be night,"
even the darkness is not dark to thee,
    the night is bright as the day;
for darkness is as light with thee."

With thee—Jesus is with us, Emmanuel! This is why Mother Teresa would say to the suffering: "Pain and suffering have come into your life, but remember pain, sorrow, suffering are but the kiss of Jesus—a sign that you have come so close to Him that He can kiss you."

When we go through the darkness of our lives believing in the Son who was sent to us, out of our hearts flow the living waters, our lives find a new meaning and vocation—fulfilling the words of Psalm 84—"Happy are they who whose strength is in you, in whose heart are the highways of Zion. As they go through the valley of Baca, they make it a place of springs." Thus, even when the believer walks through suffering and himself experiences much darkness and dryness, through Christ, he makes rivers of refreshment for others. Pope John Paul II, pray for us!

Simi Sahu is a graduate student pursuing a Master of Arts in Theological Studies at St. Vincent de Paul Regional Seminary in Boynton Beach, FL. She received her Bachelor of Science in Accountancy from The College of New Jersey, Ewing, NJ in 2011 and is a licensed Certified Public Accountant. She received the gift of her faith in Jesus Christ and love for the Holy Catholic Church through the Jesus Youth movement.

14

Rev. Mr. Kyle Bell

"In my flesh I complete what is lacking in
Christ's afflictions for the sake of his body, that
is, the Church"- *Colossians* 1:24

This text from St Paul reminds me of my
Grammy. You see, Grammy, my grandmother
on my dad's side, died a couple years ago. It
wasn't a big surprise when it happened.
Grammy had been sick for quite a while. Not
only that, but on top of the physical suffering,
Grammy had been through a lot of emotional
and spiritual suffering in the years prior. One
of her sons, my uncle, had died suddenly of a
previously-undiagnosed heart condition. One
of her other sons, my other uncle, had lost his
wife while she was in labor with their daughter,
Grammy's granddaughter. And just six months
before she got sick, Grammy's husband, my
grandpa, had passed away.

She had been through a lot.

Now, this is all on the Catholic side of my

family, and growing up I always knew Grammy as sort of a Christmas-and-Easter Catholic. But over time, as she went through that crucible of suffering, I saw something change in her. She began to pray more, she became a daily communicant, and she began to speak about Jesus as if he were a close friend. Not only that, but she influenced others. Gradually, the rest of my dad's side of the family, my aunts and uncles, started slowly coming back to the Church. One day, when I asked her about it, she didn't say a word. She just smiled and pointed to a crucifix on her wall. And it was clear: the God who identifies with suffering was now identifying with Grammy. Not only that, but the Suffering Servant, who freely entered into human suffering, had entered into hers, and was redeeming it from within, redeeming the family from within.

"In my flesh I complete what is lacking in Christ's afflictions for the sake of his body, that is, the Church."

We fear suffering so much. We fear death so much. We call it part of the human condition, and yet the Perfect Human—Jesus Christ, who shows us what true humanity at its best looks like—willingly endured the worst of suffering and death, for us. And we are mysteriously allowed to share in that, to complete what is lacking in Christ's afflictions for the sake of His body the Church. It tells me that suffering is not something to be feared.

It's something to be redeemed.

Near the end, when I went to the hospital, when I sat down next to Grammy's bed, when I grasped her hand, she looked at me and she smiled. She smiled and she told me that she was at peace, that she loved me and that she was proud of me. Then she pointed one more time to that crucifix. And I knew she was ready. In her suffering she had encountered the Suffering Christ, the God who suffered with her and redeemed her, and she was ready. She passed that night.

Suffering is not something to be feared. It's something to be redeemed. The invitation today is to ask for the grace to be more like Jesus, more like my Grammy, to complete what is lacking in Christ's afflictions for the sake of his Body, in our sufferings today.

Deacon Kyle Bell was raised a Methodist; baptized and nurtured in the faith at Wesley Memorial United Methodist Church in Tampa. By the time he went to college at Florida State University, our Lord was starting to really work on his heart. It was at FSU that he first felt a call to ministry. Upon graduation, he enrolled at Asbury Theological Seminary—a small Methodist seminary in Kentucky. Through his studies at Asbury, however, he began to fall in love with the Eucharist and the Roman Catholic Church. He enrolled in a local RCIA program and was received into the Church at the Easter Vigil in 2007. Deacon Kyle went on to receive a Masters in Theology from the Franciscan University of Steubenville, but that original call to ministry felt at FSU still tugged at his heart. He entered the seminary for the Diocese of St Petersburg and was ordained to the Transitional Diaconate on April 1, 2017. Deacon Bell will be ordained a priest on May 19, 2018.

15

Rev. Mr. Blake Britton

"The Word became flesh and dwelt among us." (Jn. 1:14) These words from the Gospel of St. John encapsulate the essence and origin of Christianity. Our God is not one who lives far away; He is not some distant deity removed from the reality of our human experience. No. He is flesh and bone; He is *Emmanuel, a "God-with-us."*

Even more astounding is the truth that God does not assume this human form begrudgingly or half-heartedly, but rather, "empties himself" fully into his creation (c.f. *Phil.* 2:7), a creation he desires to redeem and sanctify from the inside out. For, when God becomes human, the human person in turn becomes the valid and authentic expression of divine mystery.[3] In his Incarnation, his becoming flesh, humanity be-comes God's *preferred and established means*

---

[3] Hans Urs von Balthasar, *Explorations in Theology*, vol. 1, *The Word Made Flesh* (San Francisco: Ignatius Press, 1989), 70.

of self-communication. No longer will the followers of Yahweh have to fear seeing the face of God and dying. (c.f. Ex. 33:20) God has assumed a human face, *the face of Jesus Christ* and all who see his face "see the face of the Father" who loves and created them. (*Jn.* 14:9)

This complete self-emptying of God in the person of Christ pierces into *everything* that is human, even that which seems furthest removed from the concept of divinity. As a matter of fact, the one event that appears most horrific and against God is the very thing that becomes the full revelation of his glory and who he is as our Creator, namely, his torture and death upon the cross. Jesus was not murdered against his will; he was sacrificed by his choice. "No one takes my life from me, but I lay it down of my own accord." (*Jn.* 10:18) *The Lord chose the cross.* He chose to incorporate into the life of God one of the most fundamental yet frightening of human experiences: suffering.

What does this mean for those who call themselves Christians? What are the ramifications of God's decision to suffer? It is these two simple questions, inspired by a reflection upon the reality of Christ's Paschal Mystery, that St. John Paul II seeks to address in his apostolic letter, *On the Christian Meaning of*

Human Suffering. The late pontiff recognizes that suffering "is a universal theme that accompanies every man at every point on earth: in a certain sense it coexists with man in the world and thus demands to be constantly reconsidered."[4]

No one wants to suffer nor was anyone created to do so. There is something in us that rebels against it. This is completely natural. Yet, due to sin, suffering exists, and every person encounters it in some way, shape, or form in their lives. The question before us then is not will we suffer, but *how will we suffer?*

The capacity to suffer is actually a uniquely human aptitude. Animals can feel pain, but they cannot suffer. Suffering requires a certain level of consciousness which makes the person suffering aware that there must be a *reason for their suffering*; it cannot be pointless. Thus is born the timeless question of suffering: Why me? We innately desire to comprehend and place suffering within a logic, within a framework where it has purpose and intention. *This longing to understand suffering is even more*

---

[4] Pope John Paul II, *On the Christian Meaning of Human Suffering: Salvifici Doloris*, Anniversary ed. (Boston: Pauline Books & Media, 2014), 2.

important to us than avoiding it. If suffering is meaningless, then Sartre was right and life really is a hell with no exit. But we know this is not true. Our hearts tell us otherwise and no matter how hard we try to suppress or ignore the question, our humanity always shines through and thrusts itself into transcendence crying out to the heavens: WHY?! God, give my suffering purpose!

The good news is that suffering does not have to be pointless; it has been imbued with reason through the suffering of the Word of God made flesh.[5] This began in the Garden of Gethsemane when the sweat of Jesus became like that of blood. It was not the fear of the cross or death that tormented the Son; it was the chalice of rejection and hatred his Father asked him to drink to the dregs. The Son had to drink a chalice which said "No" to the Father when his whole existence had only been "Yes" to the

---

[5] In Greek, the words "reason", "logic" and "word" are all translated as *Logos*. This is the Greek word that St. John uses in the opening of his Gospel, "The Word (*Logos*) became flesh and dwelt upon us." (Jn.1:14) Thus, the Word of God is not a sentence or a book, but a Person, Jesus Christ. Anything this Word does is not only logical but becomes the source and measure of logic and rationality. Any activity of the Word is infused with reason, the best example of which is the Cross.

Father. Yet, in his accepting the Father's plea to embrace the "No," he transforms that "No" of Adam and Eve into the unchangeable "Yes" of the Son of Man. In this "taking into" himself of sin at its root, the Son now makes possible the sanctification and redemption of every act of suffering past, present, and future. All things now converge on his "by whose stripes we have been healed." *(Is.* 53:5 & 1 *Peter* 2:21) Sufferings caused by personal sins are now avenues of healing. Sufferings inflicted upon us are now opportunities for enrichment. Sufferings shared by societies are now the united activities of a communal Body of Christ.

In the end, Jesus did not come *only* to take away our sins or eliminate human tribulation. To claim such would be a reduction of the Messiah's mission. In truth, Christ comes to do so much more for his people. His love is radical, piercing deeper than a two-edged sword. *(Heb.* 4:12) He *must and only he can* enter into the depths of darkness. He *must and only he can* love us until the end. *(Jn.* 13:1) He *must and only he can* take onto himself the very reality that contradicts his nature: the rejection of the Father and the soured fruit of that rejection known as suffering. He *must and only he can* "become sin for us so that we might become children of God." (2 *Cor.* 5:21)

In so doing, he reveals himself as someone more than a god who simply deletes suffering; *he is the God who enters into it and partici-pates in it with his people here and now.* This is why we call him the God of *compassion* from the Latin *"cum"*-*"passione"* literally meaning the God who *"suffers"* -*"with"* us. How often we forget that ours is a wounded God! Jesus is sitting at the right hand of the Father at this very moment with holes in his hands, feet, and side. These wounds do not detract from his divinity, but rather are the indicators of his resurrected glory: "...see my hands. Reach out your hand and put it into my side. Stop doubting and believe." (*Jn.* 20:27) These words said by the Risen Lord to St. Thomas the Apostle are also an invitation to each of us who suffer in doubt. *God is with us; we are not orphans.* When the walls of loneliness and darkness seem to be closing in on you amidst the trials of illness, abuse, misunderstanding, emotional trauma and despair remember that these passing things do not have the final say. In the words of William Shakespeare's King Henry V, "There is some soul of goodness in things evil, would men observingly distil it out."[6]

In Christ, every suffering, temptation and ordeal can be transformed into an occasion for holiness and sainthood. By uniting our sufferings with the wounded Risen One, our travail is made dignified and meritorious. Every wincing of our body in pain or throb of our soul in heart-break becomes a conformation to the very Person of Jesus himself; he who likewise cried out in distress, "My God, my God, why have you abandoned me?" (*Matt.* 27:46)

"Jesus, I am afraid, please give me your strength!" "Lord, I am in excruciating pain, help me to suffer like you from the cross!" "O Christ, may every hurt in my life be for those who I love and all who are suffering!" These are the prayers of a soul who knows Emmanuel; these are the prayers of a Christian. St. Bonaventure captures the ideal beautifully in his classic poetic work, *The Tree of Life:*

> Who will grant me that my request should come about
> And that God will give me what I long for,
> That having been totally transpierced in

---

[6] William Shakespeare, *King Henry V*, Act IV, Scene I.

both mind and flesh,
I may be fixed with my beloved to the yoke
of the cross?[7]

My brothers and sisters, suffering is unavoidable. But bitter and pointless suffering *is* avoidable. When all is said and done there are two options before us: will we suffer alone allowing resentment and desolation to grasp us, or will we suffer with the crucified and risen One in whom "all things are made new?" (*Rev.* 21:5) Will we suffer unmindfully in despair, or suffer faithfully in Emmanuel, trusting that he is truly the God who is with us?

Let us end with a concluding prayer taken from *The Liturgy of the Hours,* hoping that these words of the Church take root in the depths of our hearts:

God our Father, the contradiction of the cross proclaims your infinite wisdom.

Help us to see that the glory of your Son is revealed in the suffering he freely accepted.

Give us faith to claim as our only glory the

---

[7] St. Bonaventure, *Tree of Life*, "Seventh Fruit: His Constancy Under Torture," 26.

cross of our Lord Jesus Christ, who lives and reigns with you and the Holy Spirit, one God, for ever and ever. Amen.[8]

Deacon Blake Britton is a seminarian for the Diocese of Orlando currently in his final year of formation for ordination to the priesthood. Born and raised in St. Cloud, Florida, he is a native of the state and looks forward to serving in Orlando as a priest. Deacon Blake is a graduate of the Osceola County School for the Arts where he majored in Vocal Performance before earning his Degree in Philosophy from St. John Vianney College Seminary in Miami. He now resides at St. Vincent de Paul Regional Seminary in Boynton Beach, Florida, where he is earning his Master's Degree in Divinity. Deacon Blake will be ordained a priest in May of 2018 for the Diocese of Orlando, Florida.

---

[8] *The Liturgy of the Hours*, Friday of the Thirty-Fourth Week in Ordinary Time, Week II.

16

Rev. Mr. Jack Knight

Luke 7:11-17

All I can hear in today's Gospel reading of Jesus healing and raising the son of a widow is that Jesus has a great sense of love and compassion toward the widow. Christ performs this miracle and with great love. And the crowds are amazed at Jesus' great power and authority and are forever transformed by His great love, by His great compassion, and His great miracle. And yet, isn't that what we desire even today, that we might be able to see Jesus' great power? We want some glimpse of hope and love amidst our suffering, here and now.

We don't suffer alone. We see how the Lord suffers voluntarily and innocently, and yet it doesn't seem to make any sense why He would choose to suffer. But there lies the crux; He chose to suffer out of and for love of us. The Lord gives us the paramount example of suffering not only by his teaching and lived out example, but by his death on the cross that leads to our redemption.

We are faced with many crosses and tribulations in our lives, whether it is an incurable illness, a loved one who has fallen away from the faith, a death of a close one, or the loss of a job. Or our suffering could be the slow suffering that occurs in the silence of our hearts doing the little things in life while following the Lord. Suffering takes many different forms in our lives, but whatever we suffer with, there remains great hope that our suffering need not go wasted. Rather we are given the opportunity to extend an invitation to the Lord to accompany us in our woundedness.

You see our Lord is not a mere thug, but rather a gentleman who is waiting an invitation into our lives. The Lord invites us today to be just like the crowds in the Gospel who are amazed at Jesus' great power and authority. We too can be forever transformed through our suffering. We too can be transformed by His great love. We too can witness the great miracle of being lifted up amidst our trials. As we receive the Lord in the Eucharist today, invite the Lord into your suffering and never be the same again.

Deacon Jack Knight is a seminarian of the Archdiocese of Atlanta, GA. He received a Bachelor of Arts (B.A.) in Philosophy and the Liberal Arts from Saint Joseph Seminary College, Saint Benedict, LA, in 2013. He spent two years serving in international missions with various groups prior to entering seminary. He also was employed as an Administrative Assistant to the Superintendent of Catholic Schools in Atlanta, GA. Presently in his final year of Theology at St. Vincent de Paul Regional Seminary, Boynton Beach, Deacon Jack will be ordained to the priesthood upon his graduation in June, 2018.

17

Rev. Mr. Jack Campbell

"ELOI, ELOI, LAMA SABACHTHANI?" My God,
My God...why have you forsaken me?

These words uttered by Jesus as he hung in anguish upon the Cross, could be the same words as any man, woman, or child suffering in a hospital bed, an abusive home...mental anguish, physical pain...suffering.

And the question must be asked...Why GOD?! I haven't done anything to deserve this...My daughter is just a child...My wife is a good woman...we have five children...How can you take her away? My husband is all I have...What will I do without him? Please God...Why?

Is God so high and mighty that he turns from us when we need him the most? It's a valid question. Almost everyone will ask it one day; if not already, when you or a loved one falls into illness, suffering, and death.

It's a valid question. And, one we have the answer for.

Bishop Sheen told a story on suffering, he spoke of two men in the same jail cell, guilty of the same crime, serving the same punishment. Both looked out of their cell window, through the iron bars...one saw mud...the other stars.

The cold fact is that we are humans, and with that, we have a human body, and this body will fail. For some quickly, and for some slowly... but we will still be in the same state of pain and suffering once our soul separates from this earthly body.

Jesus is the only human who has ever felt the pain and suffering of every soul. In his human frame, he felt all pain...He knew, all suffering. Whatever we go through, as difficult as it may be, Jesus was there...and He's still there...with us. He suffers with us, and we suffer with him.

We are united in this bond of shared suffering, and just as the prisoner saw mud, we can see mud when we discount the promise of Christ to never leave us or forsake us. We see the stars, when we live out our faith and trust in God to deliver us...to be with us...to comfort us...to know, just as the thief on the cross, that we will enter the Kingdom...enter into Paradise.

It's a valid question...to ask why. And the answer is in Christ...in his suffering...in his sacrifice...In his love. We suffer, we die... because that is our lot in life...but we live. Because our ransom has been paid. Hold on to the promise. You have not been forsaken...but tested and tried.

Deacon John (Jack) Campbell was originally born and raised in Ohio, traveled and worked as a Chef, eventually settling in Florida. He is serving the Diocese of Pensacola-Tallahassee, his "home." He is a late vocation, entering the seminary in his mid-forties, but ready and willing to follow a new path; a path that is unknown, but filled with hope, excitement and trust in God. He is in his final year of theological studies at SVdPRS and will be ordained to the priesthood in June of 2018.

18

Rev. Mr. Blake Britton

Fruit Among Thorns:
The Fruitfulness of Suffering

Every spring season, when I was a boy, my father would take me and my siblings through the woods to pick wild berries. I remember one particular time having difficulty finding any fruit and being convinced that all the bushes were barren. As I sat there staring hopelessly at one of the bushes, my dad came over and lifted up the foliage on the outside of the apparently unproductive plant. I was amazed at what I saw: hundreds of plump ripe berries in the underbrush of the shrub. "You see" my father said, "The deer and other animals only eat the berries on the outside of the bush because they are afraid of getting pricked by the thorns. So, if you're willing to get a little hurt and reach deep into the bush that is where you'll find the biggest and sweetest berries." The choicest fruits grow amidst the thorniest branches. This simple precept of nature carries within it a profound metaphor for the spiritual life.

The word "suffering" is rooted in the Proto-Indo-European suffix *–bher* which means "to carry." In its original connotation, *–bher* was associated with *fertility and the carrying of a child*. In other words, the genuine understanding of suffering, far from our reduced modern definition, does not indicate a purely negative or pointless reality. Rather, it denotes a capacity to bear fruit; there is a fecundity latent within suffering. It is not necessarily sterile. The seemingly "barren bush" of suffering hides rich fruit amongst the hiddenness of its spiked branches.

But how is this possible? How does suffering become fruitful? How do the barbs of travail come to rear the budding blossoms of grace? The answer is found in He who is the answer to all the questions of human longing: the Crucified and Pierced Messiah.

It is in the *living* Christ where suffering is made potent. *He is the one who brings the potential fruitfulness of suffering to its fullness from the Cross.* The Lord is tortured, He is mocked and condemned by His persecutors. His suffering is one truly amidst *thorns*, a crown of thorns which is embedded into His head. This Divine Bush appears barren and dying. Only the thorns of fear and hatred can be seen throughout the dense foliage of humiliation and darkness. There is no fruit...or so it seems. For, on the third day, the Father comes and lifts the underbrush of death to reveal the wondrous fruit hidden inside. Deep within the creviced earth a tomb lies empty...the Divine Bush is not dead, it is alive and overflowing with an endless produce. Christ is Risen!

It is the Crucified and Risen Lord who is our strength in suffering. As St. Macarius of Egypt reminds us, Christ takes on our flesh "and, using the Cross as His plowshare," cultivates the fields of our death and torment, breaking it open and pouring into its soil His precious blood thus providing the seed of redemption amongst the thorns of anguish.[9] This is the source of Christian hope. Nothing we experience is truly against us. All can be brought into the mission of goodness. We can dive into the chasm of darkness because we know that there is One who has already entered into it and forged the chasm of darkness into a "crossroads" with the abyss of love.

---

[9] St. Macarius, *Homily 28;* see *Liturgy of the Hours* IV, 595.

No one exemplifies this trusting confidence better than the Blessed Virgin Mary, this woman who quite literally "suffers" the Word. From the very beginning she suffers Him, nourishes Him with her own body and blood, a favor that would be returned by her Son from the Cross in thirty-three years' time. Within her womb she bore the Word who "is sharper than any two-edged sword" (Heb. 4:12), a divinely tempered blade which would eventually pierce her heart "so that the thoughts of many might be revealed." (Lk. 2:35) What are these thoughts of the many? They are *our* thoughts, the thoughts, questions, wonderments and fears of God's people of whom she is the first and most perfect. Her heart is a prism into which the Lord's singular brilliance is poured thus manifesting a spectrum where every Christian hue finds semblance. She is the Star of the Sea who points us towards the dawning light of her precious Son, the one in whom all suffering becomes gift and opportunity. Most importantly, she is the finest example of what a soul looks like who trusts God until the end. Even in the face of tragic and gut-wrenching sorrow, she stays with Jesus, never allowing despair to pillage her hope. In the end, her faith proves true and every ounce of suffering she surrendered to her Son is now the very cause of her ceaseless joy in heaven. It is for this reason that every generation calls her blessed. (Lk. 1:48)

Do we have the same confidence? What are the "thorniest" and seemingly barren parts of our hearts? Where does the Father need to reveal His Son within you? Is it despair from a physical, psychological or spiritual trauma? Where is the one place that God cannot possibly dwell because it is too ugly and covered in the rugged "underbrush" of bitterness, resentment, or self-loathing? Do you believe that God can make the choicest fruits of your soul blossom in that worst of places?

The Lord does not operate outside of or in spite of our brokenness, but through it. This is often challenging for us to believe. The humility of God is too much for us to bear; we are insulted by God's poverty. "There is no way that God can love that part of me!" "It is impossible for this suffering to be a 'gift and opportunity'. That is all just pious gibberish." In many ways, we fall into the same flaw as the ancient Greeks and Jews who saw the humility of Christ as a stumbling block and folly. (cf. 1 Cor. 1:23) It is difficult for us to imagine a God who proclaims powerlessness as power, sacrifice as life, and suffering as redemptive. Thus, we close off the very part of our life that is potentially the most beautiful. The pain remains, but unfulfilled and without purpose, a monster that feeds itself. Everything within us cries out for meaning to our plight, yet we have removed ourselves from the one Person who can actually imbue it with meaning. I believe that the Czech poet Rainer Rilke captures the sentiment lucidly in his poem *Lament*:

> Whom will you cry to heart? More and
> more lonely,
> Your path struggles on through
> incompressible humanity.
> All the more futile perhaps for keeping
> to its direction,
> Keeping on toward the future, toward
> what has been lost.
> Once. You Lamented? What was it?
> A fallen berry of jubilation, unripe.
> But, now the whole tree of my jubilation
> is breaking,
> In the storm it is breaking my slow tree
> of joy.
> Loveliest in my invisible landscape,
> You that made me more known to the
> invisible angels.[10]

---

[10] Rainer Maria Rilke, *The Selected Poetry of Rainer*

"Whom will you cry to heart?" Christians know the answer. Cry out to the One who became flesh so as to cultivate the "invisible landscape" where your "tree of joy" seeks root. The only bush that is barren in the soul is the one that the Savior has not been allowed to till. "Where sin is great [and I would add here, where suffering is great], grace abounds all the more!" (Rom. 5:20) Your suffering is not an obstacle to your freedom and happiness, it is a means to achieve it by uniting it to the sufferings of Jesus Christ. Let us strive to bear the fruits of our sufferings not allowing a single unripe berry of jubilation to fall to the ground and die.

In the end, this is only possible through prayer which is the cradle of hope. "Prayer and hope are naturally ordered towards each other. Prayer is the expression and proclamation of hope..."[11] This is especially true in regards to prayer that is sourced in the Eucharist. The sacrament of the Eucharist is a tangible reminder of the Incarnate Lord who abides with us in our sufferings, not just metaphorically but in an actual sacramental reality. The

Maria Rilke: Bilingual Edition (English and German Edition) (New York: Vintage, 1989), 137.

[11] Josef Pieper, *Faith, Hope, Love* (San Francisco: Ignatius Press, 1997), 107.

Lord cannot stand to be apart from us. This is why we have the Eucharist. It is through communicating authentically and candidly our sufferings to the Eucharistic Lord that they become sanctified and oriented towards the good. In the light of His heart in the Eucharist, all things are given meaning and shown their proper end. As we hone our gaze upon Jesus in Eucharist, the whole world is opened to us in all of its multi-faceted splendor, even if that world is as small as a hospital room or chemotherapy ward. The Lord is in these places. There is fruit among the thorns if only you have the faith to believe.

Deacon Blake Britton is a seminarian for the Diocese of Orlando currently in his final year of formation for ordination to the priesthood. Born and raised in St. Cloud, Florida, he is a native of the state and looks forward to serving in Orlando as a priest. Deacon Blake is a graduate of the Osceola County School for the Arts where he majored in Vocal Performance before earning his Degree in Philosophy from St. John Vianney College Seminary in Miami. He now resides at St. Vincent de Paul Regional Seminary in Boynton Beach, Florida, where he is earning his Master's Degree in Divinity. Deacon Blake will be ordained a priest in May of 2018 for the Diocese of Orlando, Florida.

19

On Hope

From Servais Pinckaers in *Sources of Christian Ethics* (CUA Press, 1995)

"Without the central role of suffering, the Gospel message would be incomprehensible, and there would be no way of explaining the Christian life. Even the Beatitudes turn upon various forms of suffering. It is suffering, whether physical, emotional, moral, or spiritual, that brings us in the last analysis to confront the problem of the meaning of our life and to question ourselves about our moral and religious values. It leads us to question God's goodness and, in the end his very existence. For us, suffering is the concrete shape of the problem of evil. The experience of suffering can overturn the moral values of a lifetime. . ., challenge us to a decisive existential choice: either suffering will destroy the roots of hope in us and bring us to a more or less articulate despair, or we will discover in it and beyond it new, strong values, notably Gospel values, which will engraft in us a 'hope against hope' and give us 'the courage to be'." (pp. 24-5)

20

Very Rev. Msgr. David Toups

"Seeds of Hope spread through the public
witness of the priest"

We have heard a lot about "hope and change"
this past month! But *that* "hope and change"
cannot save souls. However, you my dear brothers are the hope that can change the course
of human history, thus the title of tonight's
conference: "Seeds of Hope spread through the
public witness of the priest."

A little over six years ago my dear father died
after a very short battle with pancreatic cancer.
My dad was a man of deep faith and he faced
the end of his life with the courage and convic-
tion of a Christian. He took as his motto that of
Padre Pio: "Pray, hope, and don't worry." Isn't
that exactly what each of us should be doing on

a daily basis? As St. Paul wrote to the Romans: "Rejoice in hope, endure in affliction, persevere in prayer." (Rm. 12:12) Rejoice in hope and persevere in prayer! The Christian always lives with hope, my dad knew that his citizenship was in Heaven and that no matter what, as he walked his daily journey not knowing precisely when his impending death would come, for him "life was Christ and death was victory." (cf. Phil. 1:21-23)

Hope is the theological virtue that keeps us looking "forward to the resurrection of the dead and the life of the world to come." Hope reminds us that we are never alone, and that no matter how dark the hour may seem, we are never abandoned. When Pope Benedict XVI came for his apostolic visit to the United States in 2006 he chose as his theme: "Christ our Hope!" He also chose the topic of hope for his second encyclical letter entitled *Spes Salvi* in 2007. Pope Benedict wrote:

"When no one listens to me anymore, God still listens to me. When I can no longer talk to anyone or call upon anyone, I can always talk to God. When there is no longer anyone to help me deal with a need or expectation that goes beyond the human capacity for hope, he can help me. When I have been plunged into complete solitude ...; if I pray I am never totally alone. The late Cardinal Nguyen Van Thuan, a prisoner for thirteen years, nine of them spent in solitary confinement, has left us a precious little book: *Prayers of Hope*. During thirteen years in jail, in a situation of seemingly utter hopelessness, the fact that he could listen and speak to God became for him an increasing power of hope, which enabled him, after his release, to become for people all over the world a witness to hope—to that great hope which does not wane even in the nights of solitude." (*Spes Salvi*, 32)

Hope is the fundamental virtue that keeps us focused on the positive in the midst of seeming defeat. "Where, O death, is your victory? Where, O death, is your sting?" (I Cor. 15:55) That is why we pray daily in the Embolism of the Lord's Prayer: "as we await the blessed hope and the coming of our Savior, Jesus Christ!" *Beatam Spem* – blessed hope! We have one Savior and He will deliver us! The question we must ask ourselves regularly is, Am I living for Heaven? Is my life focused on the final goal every day?

On the pinnacle of the Basilica of St. Paul's in Rome is a beautiful marble cross with the words "*spes unica*" inserted in mosaic. The

Cross is our only hope—again think of the image of the Great Cross in St. Augustine on our Year of Faith prayer card. The Mystery of the Cross—Christ's passion, death, and resurrection—is truly our only hope. Without Christ, life is hopeless! That is why our task of priestly formation is so urgent; the world needs you to offer hope. A priestly life well lived offers just such hope to the world. We must know who we are and be firmly grounded in the faith in order to offer hope to our brothers and sisters. That is why the author of Hebrews writes, "[...] be strongly encouraged to hold fast to the hope that lies before us. This we have as an anchor of the soul, sure and firm [...]" (Heb. 6:19-19) Hope anchors us and keeps us firmly moored during the storms of life: in the face of sickness and death, in the face of loneliness and frustration, in the face of sorrow and distress it is hope that helps us to overcome, because Christ is our hope!

We spoke in the last rector's conference about our need to be credible witnesses and today we speak of our need to be hope-filled witnesses. Our Holy Father wrote, "Hope in a Christian sense is always hope for others as well. It is an active hope, in which we struggle to prevent things moving towards the 'perverse end.' It is an active hope also in the sense that we keep the world open to God. Only in this way does it continue to be a truly human hope." (*Spes Salvi*, 34) Hope is not individualistic; it is always open to other and for others. (cf. *Spes Salvi*, 28) We are to be seeds of hope in the midst of our Church and society.

I now want to take a more practical look at four ways in which we bring hope into the world and then conversely the pitfalls that can cause despair.

1) The faithful want to see something different in us. As St. Paul wrote, "Do not conform your-selves to this age but be transformed by the renewal of your mind, that you may discern what is the will of God, what is good and pleasing and perfect." (Rm. 12:2) Be trans-formed by your time in priestly formation; transformed more and more into the image and likeness of Christ himself. Remember the word for "holy" in Hebrew is *kadosh*—meaning separated. We are called to daily enter into the Holy of Holies in order to be transformed. "Prayer is the school of hope," according to Pope Benedict XVI. (*Spes Salvi*, 32) As priests and future priests, we are to foster a "monasticism of the heart;" an inner sanctum in which we encounter the living God and allow Him to form us on a daily basis. When we are

in the parish or even on vacation our schedules and daily horarium should look different from that of other people our age—do our lives revolve around God? Are they marked by times of prayer? Are we in relationship and seeking Communion with the Blessed Trinity? The heart open to this kind of ongoing conversion offers great hope to the world—when people see in us persons striving for holiness we bring them great hope!

The reverse side of this coin is when we try to be like everyone else. People really do want more from us. Whether it is our use of language, or inappropriate relationships, or the way we dress (don't be a fashion plate), or our use of alcohol, or our social activities, or any form of a worldly lifestyle. The *Code of Canon Law* reminds us, "Clerics are to follow a simple way of life and avoid anything which smacks of worldliness (*vanitatem*)." (*CIC* 282) Regarding our call to not be conformed to this age, I would like to say a few words about the use of alcohol and invite us to pay close attention to any abuse of this substance and its addictive nature. A priest who drinks heavily does not engender hope in the people of God. We heard St. Paul's admonition in Monday's liturgy that leaders not be drunkards. (Titus 1:8-9) This insidious vice can sneak up on us and bite us if we are not cautious, prudent, and moderate in our drinking. The *Catechism of the Catholic Church* reminds us that "the virtue of temperance disposes us to *avoid every kind of excess*: the abuse of food, alcohol, tobacco, or medicine." (*CCC* 2290) There is *never* a reason to have more than two to three drinks as a maximum. I pray that this is not an issue in our house of formation, but at times I have heard of occasional abuses in the past. Such abuse will be addressed in the future out of love and concern for the individual and the people of God.

2) Be present when needed for the joys and sorrows of people's lives; especially the sorrows—we offer hope for eternal life and remind them that God has not abandoned them. I think back to moments with the dying or ministering to families in ICU—what might not seem like a big deal, or what might have seemed like an inconvenience, can be life changing for the person in need. The stories I still hear from fifteen years ago from my first assignment humble me, because very often I simply do not remember these pivotal moments they experienced. Being a good priest is not rocket science, it is as easy as "just showing up;" and that self-oblation and availability we offer make all the difference in the world. Being

present in order to bring hope also can happen when we are not even trying. A priest who is in the regular habit of wearing the Roman collar will be a billboard for eternity as he goes about his daily business. Don't under-estimate the power of our priestly presence in the market-place—indeed we offer hope!

On the flip side, when we don't show up when we are needed, or when we fail to return calls from parishioners in a timely fashion we fail to offer them hope. My former parish of Christ the King was a parish that could be counted on and people deeply appreciated it. There would be times that the answering service would call us when they could not reach the neighboring parish who was being contacted. Now mind you it would make me crazy when other churches would show a lack of responsibility by not answering their line—I would later contact the pastor out of justice and find out if there was an issue as to why their call needed to be answered by us—but the point is there were persons on the other end who needed a priest and our pastoral zeal to help must override our personal comfort. Despair and distress (and a few nasty phone calls) follow when we don't respond to our people in need. There will be countless occasions when God will use you as an instrument of healing and hope for his people.

Another important moment to be present is on Sundays. Now this may sound like a no-brainer, but you might be surprised that the day that should have "all hands on deck" is not always so. When we don't show up on Sundays to greet and assist with Holy Communion we are missing a huge opportunity to be present to our family. The faithful will never get to know, love, and trust us if they only see us at the Masses we celebrate in our monthly rotation. The little things matter—you bring hope when you just show up at Mass, at meetings, at the hospital, at the Knights of Columbus Fish Fry, at school, or even at the occasional First Communion party.

3) Youth and Young Adult Ministry: Make the youth a priority—they are the hope for the future of the Church. There are occasions in which I hear of a newly ordained telling the pastor "I don't do youth ministry"—wrong answer. We do whatever the needs of our parishes are. I remember showing up to my first assignment and being told by the pastor to get on a bus the next day to drive up to Atlanta with 100 teens I had never met before. That was frightening, but the fruit of a priestly presence makes all the difference in the world when it comes to

young people. The bonds that were made with the youth on this trip have resulted in weddings, baptisms, seminarians, and a religious sister. Teens and college age students are like sponges desiring to soak up the truth. If we shun our responsibility as spiritual fathers then we will lose the battle of transforming our society. They need us to bring them hope, and their youthful zeal and unjaded innocence offers us hope in return.

When we show no interest in the New Evangelization and the new generation of young people—can you say hello to the evangelical Church down the street? A former parishioner came up to me when I first arrived and said that his daughters were all going to an evangelical youth group and that he would have so much preferred them to be exposed to the riches of our Catholic faith. My first hire was a director of youth ministry and two years later, his daughters who were beginning to drift from the Church were now leaders amongst our own youth group. We offer hope to the whole parish when they see an active and vibrant youth ministry. Funds and human resources must be allocated in order to make it happen, and the active presence of one of the priests of the parish is paramount for its success. As the newly ordained that will most likely fall to you—get ready!

4) Preach on difficult issues, but that is only after the faithful get to know you and know that you have their best interests in mind. Once you have established spiritual clout with them they will follow you, their shepherd. Now I don't mean preaching a fire-and-brimstone every week, but there are appropriate occasions throughout the year in which we must speak the truth of the Church's teaching. We now live in a nation in which the majority no longer holds to traditional Judeo-Christian values. It has become quite evident recently that the moral teachings of the Church are no longer valued by the mainstream and sadly, by many Catholics as well, whether that be on the nature of and the indissolubility of marriage between a man and a woman; contraception; abortion; euthanasia; fetal stem cell research; religious liberty, etc. You give hope to the faithful that the Church still has a moral voice when you preach the truth in love. Our vocation reminds them that we are all "here to get out of here"— i.e. to live in freedom, to draw closer to the Lord, and get to Heaven—that is where our true citizenship lies.

When the faithful don't hear the Good News preached, they get discouraged. Words of encouragement, counsel, and even at times words of challenge—all offered in love and with the Gospel message of Christ as the center bring our people great hope. When we fail to live and preach prophetically we offer the faithful no hope for the future. Our ministry is not social work; we must not cease striving to "save souls" and build up the Kingdom. We have the opportunity to bring great joy and hope or be the source of despair and distrust. *Gaudium et Spes* are the first words of the Vatican II document on the *Church in the Modern World*; *Gaudium et Spes* (Joy and Hope). If we are to make Christ and His Church relevant in today's world, we must be men of joy and hope. We bring hope to the faithful by being fully integrated men, certainly human, certainly men who make mistakes, but men who are striving to be men of faith, not drawing attention to ourselves but to Christ. We are "clay vessels," and we recognize that from the beginning Christ called a bunch of characters. *We* are comforted and given *hope* by the words of our Lord: "It was not you who chose me; it was I who chose you to go forth and bear fruit." (John 15:16)

Due to scandal in the Church, many have had their faith shaken regarding the very nature of the priesthood. While the sacraments are not dependent upon the worthiness of the minister, there is the subjective responsibility of the ordained to respond to the gift received at ordination. For the sake of God's people, priests must foster their personal character and align it with the sacramental character received at ordination that we may be credible witnesses in order that "the world may believe in him who sent us." Fr. Federico Suarez writes, "Each individual must behave in accordance with what he is. The priest, a consecrated man, has a special quality, the quality of something holy, for his sacramental consecration endows him with a sacred character. He can no longer behave as if this special quality did not exist. He is a man of God, belonging no longer to himself but to God alone." We are certainly not better than anyone else, but because of our state in life as an ordained witness to Christ, the call to holiness is elevated and the obligation is inherent to be a man of extra-ordinary virtue.

In today's world, and even in the Church, there is a temptation to despair. However, Christian hope, the theological virtue, is to be the rock of our lives. The great French writer, Georges Bernanos, once wrote about "real hope." He said that it "must be won. [We] can only attain hope through truth, at the cost of great effort and long patience...Hope is a virtue, *virtus*, strength; a heroic determination of the soul. [And] the highest form of hope is despair overcome." ("Sermon of an Agnostic on the Feast of St. Therese") St. Paul reminds us in Romans 5:3-5: "We even boast of our afflictions, knowing that affliction produces endurance, and endurance, proven character, and proven character, hope, and hope does not disappoint, because the love of God has been poured out into our hearts through the holy Spirit that has been given to us." Remain steadfast, remain in His love, "the highest form of hope is despair overcome." Christ is our hope!

As I close, I want to quote at length from a writing of the late second century called *The Letter to Diognetus*, in which the community is commended to keep their eyes on Heaven as their true homeland:

"Christians are indistinguishable from other men either by nationality, language or customs. [...]

"And yet there is something extraordinary about their lives. They live in their own countries as though they were only passing through. They play their full role as citizens, but labor under all the disabilities of aliens. Any country can be their homeland, but for them their homeland, wherever it may be, is a foreign country. [...]

"They live in the flesh, but they are not governed by the desires of the flesh. They pass their days upon earth, but they are citizens of heaven. Obedient to the laws, they yet live on a level that transcends the law. Christians love all men, but all men persecute them. Condemned because they are not understood, they are put to death, but raised to life again. They live in poverty, but enrich many; they are totally destitute, but possess an abundance of everything. They suffer dishonor, but that is their glory. They are defamed, but vindicated. A blessing is their answer to abuse, deference their response to insult. For the good they do they receive the punishment of malefactors, but even then they, rejoice, as though receiving the gift of life. [...]

"To speak in general terms, we may say that the Christian is to the world what the soul is to the body. As the soul is present in every part of the body, while remaining distinct from it, so Christians are found in all the cities of the world, but cannot be identified with the world. As the visible body contains the invisible soul, so Christians are seen living in the world, but their religious life remains unseen. The body hates the soul and wars against it, not because of any injury the soul has done it, but because of the restriction the soul places on its pleasures. Similarly, the world hates the Christians, not because they have done it any wrong, but because they are opposed to its enjoyments.

"Christians love those who hate them just as the soul loves the body and all its members despite the body's hatred. It is by the soul, enclosed within the body, that the body is held together, and similarly, it is by the Christians, detained in the world as in a prison, that the world is held together. The soul, though immortal, has a mortal dwelling place; and Christians also live for a time amidst perishable things, while awaiting the freedom from change and decay that will be theirs in heaven. As the soul benefits from the deprivation of food and drink, so Christians flourish under persecution. Such is the Christian's lofty and divinely appointed function, from which he is not permitted to excuse himself."

Now *that* is "hope and change" we can believe in, because Christ is our Hope! It is said that "hope springs Eternal," indeed hope moves us forward to eternal life. May our world see this hope proclaimed through our lives.

We now turn to our Blessed Mother in order to be fortified and encouraged, to be reminded that our citizenship is in Heaven with her Divine Son, Our Lord and Savior, Jesus Christ our King!

Mary, you are our life, our sweetness, and our HOPE.

Pray for us, O holy Mother of God; that we may be made worthy of the promises of Christ.

21

Very Rev. Msgr. David Toups

"Service vs. Being Served: Jekyll and Hyde"

I want to begin tonight with the image of a book written by Robert Louis Stephenson in 1886: *The Strange Case of Dr. Jekyll and Mr. Hyde.* According to Wikipedia:[12] "The work is commonly associated with the rare mental condition often called 'split personality', referred to in psychiatry as dissociative identity disorder, where within the same body there exists more than one distinct personality. In this case, there are two personalities within Dr. Jekyll, one apparently good and the other evil. The novella's impact is such that it has become a part of the language, with the very phrase 'Jekyll and Hyde' coming to mean a person

---

[12] "The Strange Case of Dr. Jekyll and Mr. Hyde," http://en.wikipedia.org/wiki/Strange_Case_of_Dr_Jekyll_and_Mr_Hyde

who is vastly different in moral character from one situation to the next." Jekyll and Hyde are who we want to avoid becoming in our pastoral ministry—especially in our transition from the seminary to ordination.

In other words, to go through formation and act one way for the sake of the Formation Team and then act in a contrary way once ordained because no one can tell me what to do—this is clericalism at its worst. This is what Pope Francis is referring to when he warned seminary formators about not creating "Little Monsters." So tonight I am going to present a few vignettes, painting in broad strokes, even caricatures in order to make the point. Dr. Jekyll was a well-respected and mild-mannered gentleman, but after taking a potion he was transformed into a dangerous monster that hurt others, and we certainly do not want to have such a "split personality" in our own lives.

So let's talk about the dutiful and diligent hardworking seminarian who becomes a seeming lackluster and lazy priest who shows no initiative. I hear pastors say to me that their associate does what is mandatory (i.e., shows up for Mass) but he doesn't know how to engage the parish family—thus what does it mean to show up to activities that are not mandatory? A walk through the school, visiting CCD children, a little time at coffee and donuts, basketball or volleyball game (e.g., one sporting event per season and the parishioners will think you are at everything), being in the office during office hours even when you don't have scheduled appointments; visiting various meet-ings of the Knights of Columbus, the RCIA, the Women's Guild, and various organizations even if ever so briefly. I wonder sometimes if we don't set you up for this confusion in the seminary when we make the distinction of mandatory and optional—which translates I don't have to show up. Learn as a priest/as a father to show up. Yes it takes time, but it also brings joy. The "good weariness" and "fruitful and joyful exhaustion" that Pope Francis spoke of on Holy Thursday:

This weariness in the midst of activity is a grace on which all priests can draw. (cf. *Evangelii Gaudium*, 279) And how beautiful it is! People love their priests, they want and need their shepherds! The faithful never leave us without something to do, unless we hide in our offices or go out in our cars wearing sun glasses. There is a good and healthy tiredness. It is the exhaustion of the priest who wears the smell of the sheep...but also smiles the smile of a father rejoicing in his children or grandchildren. It has nothing to do with those who wear expensive cologne and who look at others from afar and from above. (cf. ibid., 97) We are the friends of the Bridegroom: this is our joy. If Jesus is shepherding the flock in our midst, we cannot be shepherds who are glum, plaintive or, even worse, bored. The smell of the sheep and the smile of a father....Weary, yes, but with the joy of those who hear the Lord saying: "Come, O blessed of my Father." (Mt 25:34) (Homily at the Chrism Mass 2 April 2015)

Or how about that same dutiful and diligent hardworking seminarian who *seemingly* becomes lackluster and lazy because he is busy always protecting himself? I hear pastors tell me, "Don't send me a Carthusian, send me a servant." We live in a very regimented and structured environment here in the seminary and so there is a proper time for everything—in the parish, there is a proper time for nothing— what do I mean by that? In the seminary you always know when you are going to pray your Office, pray your Holy Hour, have Mass, eat your meals, make time for exercise and spend time in fraternity. In the parish, flexibility must become your middle name! One sick call to the hospital, one family crisis that shows up in the office, one angry parent who walks over from the school can shoot your whole schedule. Or do we say, "I'm sorry that is Father's nap time" (which, by the way, naps cannot be your norm!), or exercise time, or prayer time, or even day off. Learn to be flexible—make adjustments on the fly and die to self in that moment—not easy, but this is what a father does for his children. Ask parents how they do it (even the bad ones): they must sacrifice their own desires and comforts for the good of their children. That being said, I deeply want you to be men of prayer—daily Mass, Liturgy of the Hours, silent time in intimacy with the Lord— but know that it might be at a different time each day or you may need to make midstream adjustments, or even pray late at night to catch up. (I can't tell you how many times I have had late night Holy Hours and Hours of the Office a little behind the *veritas horarum*). Similarly, your health is very important to me and to the Church, but if something in our schedule has to give, it is our daily exercise—how I would love to be able to do something physical everyday but it is not realistic. If I can get 3 or 4 days a week for 30-45 minutes I am doing great. You will not have time to go to LA Fitness for an hour and a half everyday as a priest—realize this now and adjust your expectations. Your work week will be sixty to eighty hours. This is not a forty hour job—it is our vocation. While our friends work from nine to five, our work is a little more all-encompassing because this is also our family. Our friends work eight hours and then run carpool and soccer practice and housecleaning and cooking. We don't have to take kids to soccer, but sometimes we need to take a walk out to the sports field and see "our" children play (and beat St. Lawrence!). If you think of priesthood as work, the eighty hour week will exhaust you. Remember, I am counting prayer and liturgy as part of our "work day"—this is who we are, don't freak out. I recently heard from an old man the cliché: "Do what you love and you will never work a day in your life!" If we realize it is our life then we can find the joy as Pope Francis mentioned at the Chrism Mass. We are not always going to love every moment of every day, but Jesus Christ gives the meaning to all we do, and "where there is love, sacrifice is easy."

Another vignette for you is the simple seminarian who exists on very little money who becomes the worldly extravagant priest who not only liberally spends his own money, but also that of the parish. Talk about a change of gears when you are ordained. You go from having absolutely zero money to being given $30,000, of which practically all is disposable income. How easy it is to allow our spending to get out of control—buying clothes (both secular and clerical), the latest gizmos and gadgets, a constant wave of mail order catalogue boxes showing up at the rectory, overspending on the parish credit card or submitting every receipt as though we are owed everything. People often want to give us money for our services and my response is, "That is what I get paid for—I actually *do* get a salary as a priest." The truth is that we really don't need more of anything. They will often give it anyway, and so be generous in giving it back—tithe abundantly to various organizations including your own parish and alma mater! As the great Msgr. Gerry Finnegan of Venice would say, "Never, ever, ever accept money at a sick call." This is just what we do. We may get a gift at a wedding or baptism other than the parish offering, but *never* when we have gone to a house or hospital to anoint someone—I always say, just put it in the poor box next time you are at church. Remember Canon 282:

§1 Clerics are to follow a simple way of life and avoid anything which smacks of worldliness.

§2 Goods which they receive on the occasion of the exercise of an ecclesiastical office, and which are over and above what is necessary for their worthy upkeep and the fulfillment of all the duties of their state, they may well wish to use for the good of the Church and for charitable works.

Let me paint another picture of the middle-of-the-road, very healthy seminarian who leaves the seminary only to become the arch-conservative liturgical throwback to the sixteenth century. Who are you? How were you formed? Why did I never see this? Where did you come from? And, most importantly, is this what the people of God need you to be? I must admit from time to time I get blown away by this one—priests who act like they know better than their bishops, pastors, certainly the seminary in which they were trained and they come out guns blazing to change how their parish does just about everything. OK, I get the zeal, but not the imprudence and arrogance. Listen, learn, and grow into a member of the new family you are being sent to. *Please* worry more about the Latinos than your Latin!

Or how about the docile obedient seminarian who after ten years of ordination refuses to move when asked by the bishop. Really? Which part of this did he not realize is exactly what obedience entails: to serve the greatest need of our diocese as discerned by our bishop even when it is inconvenient.

Or the submarine seminarian who says all of the right things regarding celibacy to the Formation Team only to find himself in trouble from acting out later in parish ministry with a needy divorcee, a handsome young woman *or* man, a wealthy widow, or absolutely God forbid a minor! Brothers, the grass is always greener. And this area is where we usually "weary ourselves" (cf. *Evangelii Gaudium*, 277) as Pope Francis lamented at the Chrism Mass:

"But this third kind of weariness is more "self-referential": it is dissatisfaction with oneself, but not the dissatisfaction of someone who directly confronts himself and serenely acknowledges his sinfulness and his need for God's mercy, his help; such people ask for help and then move forward. Here we are speaking of a weariness associated with "wanting yet not wanting," having given up everything but continuing to yearn for the fleshpots of Egypt, toying with the illusion of being something different. I like to call this kind of weariness "flirting with spiritual worldliness." (ibid.)

When we straddle the fence and flirt with spiritual worldliness, especially in reference to celibacy, we exhaust ourselves! Pope Francis in his 2015 Message for the World Day of Prayer for Vocations[13] reminds us:

"Jesus says: "Everyone who has left home or brothers or sisters or father or mother or children or lands, for my name's sake, will receive a hundredfold, and inherit eternal life." All of this is profoundly rooted in love. The Christian vocation is first and foremost a call to love, a love which attracts us and draws us out of ourselves, "de-centering" us and triggering "an ongoing exodus out of the closed inward-looking self towards its liberation through self-giving, and thus towards authentic self-discovery and indeed the discovery of God."

I am always drawn back to Luke 9:62: "No one who sets a hand to the plow and looks to what

---

[13] Pope Francis, March 29, 2015. Available online at http://w2.vatican.va/content/francesco/en/messages/v ocations/documents/papa-francesco_20150329_52-messaggio-giornata-mondiale-vocazioni.html

was left behind is fit for the kingdom of God." And remember the great line that I have previously shared from Msgr. Preston Moss from Nassau—"Keep your hands to the plow, even when they are bleeding!"

And now to the really mundane and immature: the seminarian who cleans his room before inspection and never integrates the good stewardship behind it only to be black-balled by the priests of his diocese who do not want that slob in their rectories.

Or one more, the eager beaver who is very conscientious with his work, but who also says yes to everything outside of the parish. Someone once told their pastor, "But Msgr. Toups does this, LOL!" I just want to make clear that what the rector of a major seminary has to do is very different than an associate pastor—I leave for a meeting or a talk and there are ten other priests on campus. You leave the parish and there is maybe one left holding the bag and building up resentments toward you. Don't get me wrong, there is a time and place to appropriately get involved outside the parish for the occasional youth retreat or college campus talk, but only in dialogue with your pastor and never at the detriment of your primary community. Always be faithful to being present to your parish first.

Now is the time to learn how to be a parish priest. To learn how to prioritize and distinguish the greater good at any given time, to distinguish the difference between unstructured time and free time. In other words, if you only have the Sunday 8:00 a.m. Mass, you are not free the rest of the day to tailgate at the Jags game (except on *very* rare occasions). We must all learn to be personally responsible for the parish in which we serve: *You* will be the administration, not Keith, Fr. Remek, and Msgr. Toups; take initiative when you see a problem: when the school alarm goes off in the middle of night, it is your problem. Act the same now, this is your home. This is your parish. If you see something that needs to be fixed, fix it; if you hear an alarm going off, report it. Don't be afraid of work, laying down your life, and sacrificing for your family: "model your life on the mystery of the Lord's cross."

Ultimately, poor Dr. Jekyll longs to be free of the nagging Mr. Hyde who continues to drain him and drag him down. Don't be your own worst enemy! Be free and find points of integration all throughout your seminary career. *Understand* what you do, *imitate* what you celebrate, and *conform* your life to the mystery of the Lord's cross."

Pope Saint John Paul the Great wrote:

"[It] is vital to educate priests to have the virtues of asceticism and interior discipline, a spirit of sacrifice and self-denial, the acceptance of hard work and of the cross. These are elements of the spiritual life of the priests who are to put into practice the 'radical self-giving' proper to their vocation, following the example of Christ, who said: 'I glorified you on earth by accomplishing the work that you gave me to do' (John 17:4)." (*Pastores Dabo Vobis*, 28)

And as Pope Francis concluded his Chrism Mass Homily, so do I tonight:

"Our discipleship itself is cleansed by Jesus, so that we can rightly feel 'joyful,' 'fulfilled,' 'free of fear and guilt,' and impelled to go out 'even to the ends of the earth, to every periphery.' In this way we can bring the good news to the most abandoned, knowing that 'he is with us always, even to the end of the world." And please, let us ask for the grace to learn how to be weary, but weary in the best of ways! (2 April 2015)

Testimonials

These reflections on John Paul II's Gospel of Suffering by lay theology students and transitional deacons are pastorally-wise and theologically-rich. They shed light on the age-old question of the meaning of human suffering. With lively examples from daily life, they guide the reader to embrace the redemptive value of suffering in union with Christ for the sake of his Body, the Church.

– Archbishop J. Michael Miller, CSB, Archdiocese of Vancouver, British Columbia, Canada

In this engaging collection of homilies, Pope Francis' call for us to become missionary disciples is informed by St John Paul II's profound reflections on the mystery of human suffering. These homilies by deacons-soon-to-be-ordained-priests and lay theologians offer to us a way of relating the missionary zeal explicit in the Gospel with our own mysterious share in the Cross of our Lord Jesus.

– Bishop Kevin C. Rhoades, Bishop of Fort Wayne-South Bend, Indiana

I am grateful to the Fourth Theologians of St Vincent de Paul Regional Seminary who have shared with us their brief and deep theological reflections on human suffering. The reader will be surprised to find such wisdom in the homilies of these young men (and the reflections of two women in the class) on a reality that relates to us all.

– Most Reverend Felipe J. Estévez, S.T.D., Bishop of the Diocese of St. Augustine, Chairman of the Seminary's Board of Trustees

This collection of heartfelt and thoughtful homilies and reflections by our soon-to-be graduates offers the reader brief yet deeply theological insights into the perennial problem of suffering. I am very proud of the work they have done, and I look forward to witnessing their efficacious pastoral ministry in the years to come.

– Msgr. David L. Toups, President-Rector, St. Vincent de Paul Regional Seminary, Boynton Beach, FL

I join diverse readers who will mine gems of hope in the midst of suffering from *Diamonds in the Rough*. As a nurse, it adds another viable tool to my arsenal of empathetic care-giving for patients who suffer. As a wife, it has granted me retrospective reassurance about my beloved husband's grave suffering for months last year following invasive surgery. And as a patient myself many times over, it has helped me understand suffering as a source of hope in communion with Christ's own suffering. We need not consider suffering the end product. *Diamonds in the Rough* encourages our acceptance of the mystery of suffering, inviting those who suffer to become participants in God's redemptive love.

– Diane Haight, RN, BIS, MA

This set of Homilies on the Theology of Suffering based upon *Salvifici Doloris*, prepared by students of the medical ethics course at Saint Vincent de Paul Regional Seminary, is a sign of pastoral commitment to the suffering world we are called to serve. This book will be a wonderful resource for the ministry of preaching to the people of God who face challenging situations where it is difficult to discover the provident presence of our Good God.

– Fr. Jaime E. Robledo, PSS, formation adviser, spiritual director, and moral theologian at St. Patrick's Seminary and University, Menlo Park, California

63614200R00092

Made in the USA
Middletown, DE
03 February 2018